TRUMP

THE SAGA OF AMERICA'S MOST POWERFUL REAL ESTATE BARON

TRUMP

THE SAGA OF AMERICA'S MOST POWERFUL REAL ESTATE BARON

by JEROME TUCCILLE

BeardBooks
Washington, D.C.

**TO THE MEMORY OF
NORMAN BASILE**

CONTENTS

ACKNOWLEDGMENTS and an Author's Note

I would like to thank several people who were especially helpful to me in researching this book: Geri Shapiro, who served as an unpaid but indefatigable research assistant; Arlene Ethevenon, who was always on the alert for breaking stories on Donald Trump that I could not keep up with; June Curley, who provided me with information not obtainable from any other source; my son, Jerome D. Tuccille, who helped me gather some of the initial research material; friends within the real estate industry who requested anonymity; others who also chose to remain nameless but helped me track down difficult-to-locate addresses and phone numbers, and who provided background information on the Trump family not available from published material.

Researching this book turned out to be an adventure in itself that made the actual writing of it almost anticlimactic by comparison. Since no previous book had been written about the Trump family, I had to literally turn myself into a detective to get the information I needed.

The published record tends to be spotty and incomplete. Donald Trump is a master of self-promotion and publicity. Many famous people tend to be, to one extent or another, but it makes the job of research difficult.

To begin with I read all the published information on the Trump family that I could locate, including back issues of *The New York Times* going back as far as 1936. Other articles that were particularly valuable were: "The Men Who Own New York" by Nicholas Pileggi, *New York Magazine* (May 19, 1980); "Trumping the Town" by Marie Brenner, *New York Magazine* (November 17, 1980); "The Expanding Empire of Donald Trump" by William E. Geist, *The New York Times Magazine* (April 8, 1984); "Holding All the Cards" by Lawrence J. Tell, *Barron's* (August 6, 1984); "They're Loaded with Trump Cards" by Ralph Wiley, *Sports Illustrated* (March 5, 1984); "The Forbes Four Hundred," *Forbes* (October 1, 1984); "Delayed New York Housing Project Shows Problems of Urban Ventures" by Joanne Lipman, *The Wall Street Journal* (September 26, 1984); "Plan for 150-Story Building Faces Some Serious Problems" by Robert Guenther, *The Wall Street Journal* (August 29, 1984); "Supertall Buildings Called Just a Dream Away" by Rick Hampson, *Southern Connecticut Newspapers* (October 21, 1984); "Trump Sues a Copycat," *Manhattan, Inc.* (September 1984); "All Power, No Lunch" by Ron Rosenbaum, *Manhattan, Inc.* (November 1984); "New Game Plan," *Time* (September 3, 1984); "What's Causing the Gyrations at Holiday Inns" by Gene Marcial, *Business Week* (September 17, 1984); "Trumping the Competition" by Loring Leifer, *Interiors* (June 1984).

Keeping current with articles about Donald Trump remained an ongoing process as the book was being written. Once the earlier background material was digested, however, then the detailed detective work began in earnest. My first interview was with Colonel Theodore Dobias, Donald's baseball coach at the New York Military Academy. This was followed up by a visit to the academy in Cornwall-on-Hudson where I was informed by the staff that no further cooperation would be given until I had received official approval from Donald to write the book. I was permitted to go through old issues of "The Ramble," the school newspaper, as well as the yearbooks where Donald Trump's home address (previously unpublished) and other personal information were contained.

At this point I had already written letters to Donald Trump at his office in New York and to his father, Fred Trump, at his Brooklyn office, stating my intention to write the biography. Fred referred all questions to Donald. During conversations with Donald Trump's secretary, she informed me that the Trumps preferred that the book not be written. I told her that I was proceeding, and still hoped to get Donald's cooperation on the project. She said she would discuss the matter further with him and get back to me. I followed this up with more letters to both Donald and his family.

My next interview was with Elizabeth Trump, Donald's sister, who was friendly and informative over the phone. She provided me with background information on herself and the family, including birth data and other details. She declined to discuss her late brother Fred, saying that she was "not at liberty to do so." Until this time, little was known about Fred other than the fact that he was Donald's older brother and had died a few years earlier. I made a tentative appointment to meet with Elizabeth for a follow-up interview, but the next time I called she told me that she could not speak to me again until she had first cleared it with Donald.

After obtaining the family's phone number in Jamaica Estates, I called and spoke to Donald's mother. Mrs. Trump spoke briefly before referring additional questions to her husband. At the same time I was in touch with Donald's office, keeping him informed by letter of what I was doing and discussing the book with his secretary. Again, she told me that Donald wanted to consider the matter further and would get back to me. I was able to interview several of the family's neighbors in Jamaica Estates, some of whom were very helpful. My most fortuitous meeting was with a family associate who provided information about Donald's early years and those of his brothers and sisters. This was especially valuable since nothing had been written to date on the subject. The most sensitive area concerned Fred Trump, Jr. My biggest problem here was handling the material properly without causing undue anguish to the family.

My next visit was to Trump Tower, where I interviewed some of the retail tenants, including Helen Murphy of Elan, who did the landscaping in the building. My research assistant was very helpful in this regard, too, interviewing other tenants for me. Still, I kept Donald Trump informed of the progress I was making and discussed the book over the telephone with his secretary. According to her, the family preferred that I drop the project but would consider my request in further detail and get back to me. I offered to send Donald copies of my previous books if that would help, and she said she would let me know.

My next call was to the Marble Collegiate Church, where Donald and Ivana had been married by Dr. Norman Vincent Peale. I was able to get the date of their wedding, birth data, and Ivana's maiden name, which had never been published before. I also got the couple's home phone number in Greenwich from a different source, and spoke to Ivana over the telephone. She was friendly, not revealing too much, but she did give me some background material on herself as well as the name of the modeling agency she worked for in Montreal. I was able to interview the director of this agency, who verified much that she told me and was generally helpful. Other people I interviewed at this time included realtors who had done business with the Trump family going back to the late sixties and early seventies.

At this time I also wrote a letter to Linda Trump, the ex-wife of Fred, Jr., sending copies of the letter to Donald and his father. I had learned of her existence, her address, and phone number from a source who cannot be identified. When neither she nor the Trump family

responded to my letter, I called her up and spoke to her on the telephone. She, too, was friendly and expressed surprise that I was able
to track her down. But she declined to let me interview her, saying
that she would have to check with the Trump family before talking
further to me. I also spoke to Donald's secretary, who acknowledged
receipt of this letter and said she would be getting back to me.

My next visits were to Wharton on the University of Pennsylvania
campus, where Donald attended college, and to Harrah's at Trump
Plaza in Atlantic City. In both places I was able to talk with a number
of people who provided me with additional information. A most startling episode occurred on a day in November 1984, when I placed
phone calls to Parks Commissioner Henry J. Stern; Robert F. Wagner,
Jr.; Abraham Beame; Hugh Carey; and Samuel Lindenbaum, one of
Donald's lawyers.

When I called Stern's office, a woman answered the phone and I
gave my name.

"Oh," she said. "You're the one who's writing the book."

"How did you know that?"

"I make it my business to know what's going on in the publishing
world," said she.

"But we haven't publicized the book yet," I said. "You must have
gotten word from the Trump people."

"Not necessarily," she said. "I'll have Commissioner Stern return
your call."

I next spoke to attorney Lindenbaum, who said he would get back
to me after he spoke to Donald, and to Abraham Beame, who said the
same thing. The other people on the list did not return my calls.

Five minutes later the phone rang in my office. "This is John Baron
of the Trump organization," the caller identified himself. "I understand
you've been calling people all over town harassing them and misrep-
resenting yourself."

"Nonsense," I answered in somewhat stronger language. "I've kept

Donald informed every step of the way about the book. I still hope to see him."

"You've already been told that Donald doesn't want a book written about him," said Baron. "He doesn't like publicity."

"The book's being written anyway," I said. "I thought it would be best for everybody if we at least got together and cleared the air a bit. I've offered to send him anything he wants to see beforehand."

"I'll tell you what," said Baron. "Why don't you send me a copy of your last book and maybe a few other things. I think I can get you an interview with Donald."

"I appreciate it," I said, and dropped off the material the following day. Baron never got back to me, and subsequent phone calls to him, Donald, and Donald's brother Robert were not returned.

I next interviewed Der Scutt, the architect for Trump Tower and the Grand Hyatt, who turned out to be helpful and informative. He seems genuinely fond of Donald and apparently thinks very highly of him. The same is true of C. A. Kondylis, another of Donald's architects, as well as Irving Fischer of HRH Construction, which did the work on Trump Plaza, both of whom I interviewed by phone.

Every effort was made to double-check the information that appears in *TRUMP: The Saga of America's Most Powerful Real Estate Baron* to avoid any possibility of error. Material that could not be verified has been omitted. All the quotations used in the book are carefully documented; some have been altered very slightly for the sake of clarity or grammatical considerations.

To all those who cooperated in any way in the research of this book, I can only say, "Thank you very much." To those who did not, for one reason or another, I harbor no ill will. The final product is mine, and I take full responsibility for it.

PROLOGUE

Saturday, November 21, 1964, was a cold, sunny day in New York City. By eleven o'clock in the morning thousands of cheering New Yorkers had gathered on both the Brooklyn and the Staten Island sides of the Verrazano-Narrows Bridge to witness the ribbon-cutting ceremony marking the grand opening of the span. The 6,690-foot bridge had been built over a period of five years at a cost of $325 million. Three ironworkers fell to their deaths during its construction. The two towers on the bridge soared seventy feet into the sky, lending the structure a truly majestic air. President Lyndon Johnson sent a telegram on the occasion to Mayor Robert F. Wagner describing the Verrazano-Narrows Bridge as "a structure of breathtaking beauty and super engineering." Among the invited guests on hand, not too far removed from the main dignitaries at center stage, were New York real estate developer Fred C. Trump and his eighteen-year-old son Donald.

Not everyone pressing against the barricades at the 92nd Street overpass in Brooklyn and the toll plaza in Staten Island was in a festive mood. A group of teenagers had joined the throng to protest the lack of a footpath on the bridge. One of the banners they raised above their heads read, "Are Feet Obsolete?" Also protesting the occasion was a delegation from the ironworkers union that had built the bridge. Its spokesman said they were unhappy because they were the ones who actually erected the span "bolt by bolt," suffering loss of life in the process, and they were not invited to the ceremony.

In the water beneath the graceful steel arch linking these two New York City boroughs, the liner *United States* passed slowly, returning from drydock in Virginia. Scores of smaller vessels surrounded the *United States*, flags flapping in the brisk wind, cannons booming and whistles tooting. With bands playing patriotic music, stirring up the already excited multitudes, Robert Moses, chairman of the Triborough Bridge and Tunnel Authority, strode to the microphone to give the opening speech. On the dais with him were Nelson Rockefeller, governor of New York; Ambassador Sergio Fenoaltea of Italy; Abe Stark, borough president of Brooklyn; Mayor Wagner; Francis Cardinal Spellman of the Archdiocese of New York; and the modest, shy, eighty-five-year-old designer of the bridge, Othmar H. Ammann.

"I now ask that one of the significant great men of our time— modest, unassuming, and too often overlooked on such grandiose occasions—stand up and be recognized," boomed Moses's amplified voice, according to a *New York Times* story of November 22, 1964.

Ammann rose somewhat reluctantly, his still-brown hair whipping in the wind, and faced the crowds self-consciously.

"It may be that in the midst of so many celebrities," Moses, the power broker, continued, "you don't even know who he is. My friends, I ask that you now look upon the greatest living bridge engineer, perhaps the greatest of all time. A Swiss who has lived and labored magnificently sixty years in this country and is still active, the designer of the Verrazano-Narrows Bridge, respected throughout the world and regarded here with deep affection."

If the crowd failed to identify the great engineer prior to Mr. Moses's introduction, it certainly was no better informed following it. In the course of his brief but flowery acknowledgment of Mr. Ammann's contribution, the redoubtable Robert Moses neglected to mention the man's name. When the somewhat bewildered gentleman returned to his seat, someone turned around and asked him.

"How do you feel?"

"Oh, as I feel every day," Othmar H. Ammann replied in some embarrassment.

Finally at 3:00 P.M. when all the purple political rhetoric had been carried away in the wind, the dignitaries approached the ribbon with gold scissors in their hands. Governor Rockefeller was the first one to snip, and as the crowd exploded with a roar the first car rolled ahead onto the virgin span. It was a pale blue Cadillac convertible, rented especially for the occasion, and it was driven by a twenty-two-year-old Brooklynite in a rented tuxedo. With an impish grin on his face appropriate for the festivities, he said that he had parked in front of the Staten Island toll booth for a week to earn the distinction of being the first one to cross over the bridge.

For young Donald Trump observing the proceedings at his father's side, it was a vivid learning experience that he referred to many times during the next two decades. To a great extent it helped shape his philosophy and his style of operation.

"I realized then and there that if you let people treat you how they want, you'll be made a fool," Donald said to Howard Blum of *The New York Times* in an August 1980 interview. "I realized then and there something I would never forget: I don't want to be made anybody's sucker."

17

Donald must have made a conscious decision that day in 1964 to make sure his name was prominently stamped on everything he built. No one would ever forget his name at a dedication ceremony.

Stamping his name on buildings has been very much the Trump style ever since that cold November day. His successes in the major leagues of American real estate were legendary by the time he was in his mid-thirties. In a very brief period, he has managed to take a $40-million business built by his father and expand it into an empire worth well over a billion dollars. He has captured headlines all over the world with his construction of Trump Tower, a monumental commercial and residential pleasure palace on New York's Fifth Avenue; Trump Plaza, a Miami Beach-style apartment complex on the city's upper eastside; Harrah's at the other Trump Plaza, a quarter-billion-dollar glittering gambling casino in Atlantic City; the Grand Hyatt, a towering glass-and-steel superhotel atop New York's Grand Central Terminal; as well as with this foray into professional sports with the purchase of the New Jersey Generals and his anticipated venture into the world of entertainment with a television network.

So celebrated had Donald Trump become by the time he reached his thirty-eighth birthday that even the projects he failed to consummate were the subjects of great controversy. These included the castle in honor of himself, complete with moat and drawbridge, that he talked of erecting in the middle of Manhattan; the mammoth convention center on land formerly owned by Penn Central that he never built; and the 150-story tower he has been talking about putting up on landfill in the East River that would reclaim the title of "The World's Tallest Building" from Chicago's Sears Tower.

Partly by design, and partly because of his natural flamboyance, Donald Trump has emerged as one of the most powerful and controversial figures on the American scene today. Still in his thirties, he invites careful scrutiny because of his association with other controversial people such as attorney Roy Cohn, and his apparently special relationship with politicians including: Abraham Beame, former mayor of New York City; Hugh Carey, former governor of New York State; Thomas Kean, governor of New Jersey; and President Ronald Reagan. His social life with his glamorous wife has brought him to a point of acceptance by prominent members of society—an acceptance he has been seeking most of his life.

By his own admission, according to an article in *New York Magazine* on November 17, 1980, he has "... done everything so fast, done deals that it would have taken an older man a lifetime to do, if he could ever get them done. I just wonder sometimes whether I should have spread these deals over my entire life ... Maybe it was a mistake to have raced through it all so fast."

When Donald Trump turned thirty-eight in August 1984, he showed no signs that he was thinking of slowing down. Quite the contrary. Brian J. Strum, senior vice-president of Prudential, one of his close business associates, commented that he had at least "... eighteen new irons in the fire." With all the money he could possibly spend in fifteen lifetimes, with more spectacular commercial successes to his credit than most mere human beings ever dream of achieving, Donald J. Trump is still a young man with the greater part of his adult life waiting to be lived. A good deal has been written about him and his family during the past few years, some of it harmless exaggeration disseminated by Trump himself. In addition to being the most dynamic real estate baron in American today, and certainly the youngest, Donald Trump is also his own best public relations agent and creator of his own mythology. He is a firm believer in telling the press and the public what he wants to see in print, then sitting back as the body of legend continues to grow.

This book, as already mentioned, was written after an intense period of investigation that included dozens of interviews. It was done with the full knowledge of the Trump family and the cooperation of some of its members and associates, though not with their official approval. It is the first complete and detailed account of the family's history, focusing of course on Donald Trump, the unquestioned head of the Trump organization today.

The saga of Donald J. Trump is, to a considerable extent, the story of contemporary America—its values, its tastes, the look and feel of its bulging cities. To understand this unique American one needs to go back some distance in time, back to the family roots in a sprawling borough across the river from Manhattan.

Part One

THE ROOTS OF EMPIRE

1

Hillside Avenue in Queens is a long stretch of rundown bars, pizza parlors, real estate offices, check-cashing stores, hair-cutting salons known as "beauty parlors," and Chinese restaurants with menus from which you can still order items from columns A and B. Many of the people you see strolling along Hillside Avenue today are black and a fair number of the signs above the stores are in Spanish, attesting to the changing complexion of the neighborhood over the past couple of decades or so. But Hillside was a working-class neighborhood even back in the 1930s and 1940s; it is just that most of the residents in those days were of Italian, Irish, and German descent.

Adjoining Hillside Avenue, yet separated from it by an invisible but very real demarcation line, is a different kind of neighborhood. As one turns north off Hillside onto Midland Parkway, the change in environment is instant and dramatic. It is almost as though one has

23

entered a completely new world. Even today Jamaica Estates is a lush, exclusive enclave within the city pressed in by signs of spreading urban decay.

Midland Parkway is a wide, inviting boulevard lined with trees on both sides. The houses are large and well-tended, and the grounds around them are landscaped with flower gardens and trimmed hedges. The illusion of suburban tranquility is shattered, however, by the warning signs prominently displayed on the front doors. To eliminate any doubt in the minds of would-be intruders, residents of Jamaica Estates advertise that their homes are protected by alarm systems.

The Trump house is one of the largest and most impressive on the boulevard. It is set back from the street behind a phalanx of trees and a footpath that winds through a cluster of hedges and thick foliage. The three-story brick mansion has a Jeffersonian look to it. The colonnaded portico above the entrance and the black jockeys on the front lawn seem more in keeping with the Virginia countryside than with the exigencies of urban life. This quaint touch of gentility in New York City was created by Fred Trump, the patriarch of the family, as were many of the other homes in Jamaica Estates. This is the house that Donald Trump was raised in, along with his two older sisters, Maryanne and Elizabeth, his older brother Fred, Jr., and his younger brother Robert. The Trumps were of the city, yet at the same time apart from it, insulated against its harsher realities by their father's circumstances.

2

Frederick Charles Trump was born in New Jersey on October 11, 1905. His father was a hard-drinking restaurant owner who died when young Fritz was only eleven. His mother managed to find enough work as a seamstress to pay the rent and put food on the table, but it was basically a harsh existence for both of them. Their life was devoid of luxuries, and bare necessities were obtained only by struggle and long hours of labor. Fritz would have remembered his Swedish-born father as a hard and remote man, toughened by a life filled with deprivation; it was his mother to whom he was close and who strongly influenced him. She was abstemious where his father was not. She was a God-fearing Protestant where his father seemed, to some, to be communicating with the devil himself at times. It was his mother's ethic of hard work and self-discipline that permeated young Fred's spirit and became an integral part of his nature.

While he was still in high school, Fred supplemented his mother's income by working as what was referred to in those days as a "horse's helper." In the cold winter months when the horses could not pull their heavy loads up the icy slopes to the homes under construction, the contractors employed sturdy young boys like Fred to do the job instead. In his early teens he carted heavy loads of lumber up the hills to the homesites along with a dozen other ragtag kids—a spectacle to rival a scene from an American version of *Oliver Twist*. Later Fred became a full-fledged carpenter, then attended the Pratt Institute in Brooklyn, where he studied blueprint reading, mechanical drawing, and other construction-related subjects.

His first venture as an entrepreneur occurred in 1923 when he formed his own company, called Elizabeth Trump and Son, since he was not yet old enough to sign legally binding documents or even his own checks. The first house he built was a one-family dwelling in the Woodhaven section of Queens. He sold it immediately and used the profit to build two more houses in Queens Village which were followed by nineteen others in Hollis. These houses were put up at a cost of $4,000 to $5,000 apiece, depending on the weather and the availability of material, and then sold for $7,500. Within a few short years, Fred Trump was already sprinkling his uniquely styled "modern" brick houses liberally around Queens—three here, five there, twenty more in a self-contained development somewhere else. To a great extent he was pioneering a new concept in urban living: tastefully designed suburban-style houses within city limits. He was creating whole minivillages, communities within communities, with his clustered arrangement of tidy homes in a concentrated area. Most were made of brick, most were surrounded by trees and greenery, and an appearance of quality, even "class," was made available to wage earners who otherwise could not have afforded them. Queens was beginning to take on a new look and a reputation as New York City's premier suburban borough, largely through the efforts of a driven Swedish-American barely into his twenties. Trump's houses were immediate best-sellers to hundreds of New Yorkers who clamored for a touch of Westchester County in the city, and within a very short period the days of deprivation were a thing of the past for the young builder and his hard-working mother, Elizabeth.

In 1929 Fred Trump carried his vision a step further with the construction of the first houses in the area that would eventually evolve into Jamaica Estates. For six years he had prospered by building houses for upwardly mobile middle-class Americans. Now he would create real luxury dwellings, some might even call them mansions, for those who had already made it. If Woodhaven, Hollis, Queens Village, and Bellaire provided a taste of quality for New York's teachers, firemen, insurance salesmen, and retail merchants, Jamaica Estates would show the city's judges, politicians, surgeons, and racketeers what real luxury was all about. Midland Parkway and the near-lying streets between Union Turnpike on the north and Hillside Avenue on the south soon became an enclave filled with three-story colonials, five-bedroom mock Tudors, four-bathroom Victorians, and other posh residences on beautifully landscaped acreage with plenty of shrubbery all around to ensure privacy. One did not live in Jamaica Estates, the saying went—one *resided* there in manorial elegance appropriate for the accomplished few. Fred Trump did not build all the homes in Jamaica Estates, but he built enough to lay his claim to being the area's first pioneer as well as one of its wealthiest residents.

3

The Depression of the 1930s brought his building activities to an abrupt halt, but Fred Trump was able to survive by constructing a self-service supermarket in Woodhaven. Victims of economic hardship could purchase food and other staples more cheaply there than at the neighborhood grocery store, and Fred demonstrated once again that he was able to provide the public with what it needed for less money than his competition could and still make a profit for himself. His son Donald would build on that in dramatic fashion in a later era.

Fred anticipated what was to come as well as any other real estate developer in the country. Until now he had grown rich building houses for the middle and upper-middle classes. In the mid-1930s, a full ten years before the advent of Levittown and other low-cost housing developments, he directed his attention to the low end of the economic scale with the construction of a group of $3,900-houses in the East

Flatbush section of Brooklyn. He not only changed direction economically, he changed his sphere of operation to the neighboring borough
as well. He read the handwriting on the wall—the Roaring Twenties
were over, Depression was a lingering fact of life. He would move
along with the tide.

It did not take him long to get going. In 1936 Fred Trump received
FHA approval to develop the old circus grounds at Clarendon Road
from East 40th to 42nd streets as a homesite for low-income families.
Under the terms of the agreement, he and his partner Charles O'Malley
would build four hundred houses in the area. He also began to spend
time at the Madison Club in Brooklyn, and to contribute to candidates
of the Brooklyn machine running for office. Working with the government in its program to provide housing for the homeless of the
Depression was in a sense a public service. But some of these FHA-
sponsored projects were alleged by the U.S. Attorney General to have
turned into sweetheart deals for well-connected builders. The government guaranteed them against losses, and profit could be hidden in the
financing. (It should be noted that Fred Trump, Sr., was never formally
charged.)

Fred's personal life also veered in a new direction at this time. For
twelve years he had been building and amassing a fortune, too busy
with the rigors of the construction trade to spend much time on social
activity. But in 1935 he paused long enough to marry an attractive
Scottish girl named Mary MacLeod whose thick Northumbrian burr
was still noticeable during a conversation I had with her in 1984. Fred
saw in Mary many of the same virtues possessed by his mother: thrift,
a dedication to hard work and industry, and a firm belief in God and
Christian fundamentalism. Their first child, a girl, was born two years
later and named Maryanne. Fred may have been disappointed that his
wife had failed to present him with a boy, a namesake who would take
his rightful place in his father's business when he was ready. If this
were so, he was not disappointed a year later when Mary gave birth

to their first son on October 14, 1938. It was decided beforehand that he would be named Fred, Jr.

Now he had a son. Freddie. Freddie would be just like his father. Tough. Hard-working. Fred would teach Freddie what life was all about. He would prepare him for the rough-and-tumble world of business and politics. Freddie—and for that matter, his daughter—would not be pampered and coddled like so many offspring of the rich. Fred Trump was a self-made man who had risen from poverty on his own merits and built his fortune. Young Fred would be taught "how to earn a buck."

"Life's a competition," said Fred Trump in a *New York Magazine* article of November 17, 1980. "I brought my kids up in a competitive environment."

No, life for Freddie would not be a piece of cake. The boy would grow up to be tough and hard-working and take his natural place in the family business. He would be just like his old man. At least that was the plan.

4

When a second daughter, Elizabeth, was born on April 10, 1942, World War II was underway and Fred Trump had already built over 2,500 homes scattered throughout Queens and Brooklyn. On April 12, Fred announced his plans to build the 296-unit Talbot Park apartments for military personnel in Norfolk, Virginia, with another contractor, James Rosatti. The war years found him putting up temporary housing for shipyard workers and naval officers in other parts of Virginia and in Pennsylvania.

In 1946, when the war was over and government funding to house the nation's military personnel began to dry up, Fred Trump once again redirected his efforts to the kind of building he loved best. Now he would do for Brooklyn what he had done for the neighboring borough of Queens two decades earlier. He would fill its streets, avenues, and boulevards with the types of houses that were his trademark: quality, tastefully designed brick homes at affordable prices for the battalions of discharged soldiers and sailors who were returning to civilian life.

These were attached one- and two-family brick houses priced between $9,500 and $12,500. Trump's "deluxe" models—facing the water—were going for a whopping $16,500. Many of them were being built with below-street-level basements that could be "finished" into family rooms or party rooms, a new concept in home building providing homeowners with the ability to expand into "extra space" within their homes without putting on an "addition." Fred made his final break from the war effort at this time, too, when he sold his Talbot Park apartments for an undisclosed amount of cash plus a seller's mortgage of $1.1 million.

Nineteen forty-six was a banner year for Fred Trump on the homefront as well. His growing family already numbered two daughters, Maryanne and Elizabeth, and a son, Fred, Jr. In August another son was born to Fred and Mary.

They named him Donald John.

5

A discordant note in Fred Trump's life at this stage was the growing awareness that his namesake, young Freddie, the son who was going to be just like his old man, was not developing according to the script. Fred would bring the boy to his office, out at the end of Avenue Z in the Coney Island section of Brooklyn, and would take him to visit construction sites so he could see firsthand the kind of work his father was doing. It was almost as though Fred was determined to impose his will on his firstborn son by surrounding him with himself, his works. The child was to become a replica of his father in reality as well as name. Freddie, one might say, was overwhelmed.

Given his own upbringing and background, Fred could not help being a domineering father. Dealing with the sensibilities of a growing boy, particularly one who carried his name and was therefore expected to be an extension of himself, was alien to his nature.

Maryanne, on the other hand, had no such demands put on her. She was a girl and therefore not expected to follow in her father's footsteps—or even to amount to much at all. But Maryanne was smart, tough, and independent, and she had the luxury of growing up free of her father's attempts to redirect her natural inclinations. She was definitely her father's girl in many ways. She had his quick mind, his ambition, and his sense of mission. She knew at an early age that she would go on to become successful at something, not her father's business but a career of her own choosing. The younger girl, Elizabeth, was more like her mother—sweet, trusting, with a tolerant disposition that counterbalanced Fred's gruff and impatient nature.

And then there was Donald John. Donald was a round, fleshy baby who howled up a storm from the day he was born. A true Leo. Fred regarded him with some amusement, but his disappointment with Freddie prevented him from putting too much hope in his younger son. Or in the fifth and final child, born in August 1948, a boy named Robert.

So with a growing family to provide for, Fred devoted himself to his labors with even greater intensity than before. He felt that first the Depression and then the war had somehow derailed him from his appointed course and caused him to lose valuable time. So he proceeded to branch across the bay into Staten Island, erecting one- and two-family houses as quickly as he could buy up the land. In 1948 he began the first of several large-scale apartment developments built with government-backed FHA loans; these would occupy much of his time over the next couple of decades.

His first apartment complex, started in 1948, was the 1,400-unit Shore Haven Apartments just off the Belt Parkway overlooking the water in Bensonhurst. The development was an immediate sell-out, with all the apartments occupied before the mud was fully cemented over. The profit from this deal was sufficient incentive for Fred to take on an even grander project, the 1,900-unit Beach Haven Aprartments, also located near the Belt Parkway but a bit further to the east in Brighton Beach.

At forty-four, Fred's daily schedule found him spending several hours at various projects that he had under construction, and the rest of the day and evening in his Avenue Z office, grabbing a sandwich while he argued prices with contractors over the phone or negotiated a deal at his desk. He rarely took notes. His ability to store the myriad details of a deal in his head and recall them years later without error amazed even the hardboiled veterans of the real estate trade who did business with him.

As a new decade unfolded, Fred Trump was doing what he loved best. He had progressed from building two-story brick houses in Queens to erecting high-rise apartment buildings. He was in the prime of his life. On top of the world.

6

Aside from a winter vacation at The Breakers in Florida and a week in the summer at Grossinger's or The Concord in the Catskills, family life at the Trump home centered around business. Such preoccupation extended into their social life too. There were no social pretensions for the children of Fred Trump, no matter how much money he had or would ever make. Theirs was a world of political dinners, fund-raising affairs for people like Robert F. Wagner—who was New York City's Tax Commissioner, its Commissioner of Housing and Building, and Chairman of the City Planning Commission before he was elected mayor in 1953—and Robert Moses—who was perhaps even more powerful than New York's mayors for more than thirty years—and other bureaucrats with any influence over the tax laws, particularly as they affected real estate developers. Entertainment at home was also mostly business-related, with a sprinkling of judges, lawyers, and political aspirants seated around the dining-room table. Donald and the other Trump children heard "tax abatement" before algebra. Donald would never forget.

Despite the fact that Fred always insisted his offspring grow up unspoiled and knowing "how to make a buck," unlike many of the other rich kids in their community, such prescriptions could be carried only so far. Growing up in a plantation-era mansion with more rooms than they could count was a daily reminder that they *were* different. Not like other city kids. Maryanne was driven every day to the Kew Forest School, a small private school on Union Turnpike just on the edge of Forest Hills, which is an even more exclusive community than Jamaica Estates. Fred, Jr. and Elizabeth also attended private schools in the vicinity, and Donald and his younger brother, Robert, were enrolled in Kew Forest. Even the religious training was no ordinary affair. Fred and Mary Trump were members of the Marble Collegiate Church, the imposing and somewhat medieval stone structure on 29th Street and Fifth Avenue in Manhattan, the minister of which was Dr. Norman Vincent Peale, whose best-selling book, *The Power of Positive Thinking*, made him an instant celebrity in the early 1950s.

By this time it had also become apparent that if Fred, Jr. was not quite the son his father had hoped for, young Donald was perhaps a bit more than he could handle. He competed with his older brother for his father's attention in the most determined ways. He howled for no apparent reason, evidently to let his father know that he was there. He refused to play second fiddle to his older siblings, insisted on being the center of attention. Where Fred, Jr. could not wait to get home from the mandatory excursions to assorted construction sites, Donald loved to get his shoes muddy tromping through them, playing with bricks, planks, nails, and other paraphernalia of the trade. If only the boys had been born in reverse order . . . it would have been much easier to accept . . .

Donald's exuberance carried over into his school life. The boy was a hyper child, overflowing with energy and a need to assert himself among his fellow students. Fred was on the board of directors of the Kew Forest School, and was one of its most generous financial supporters. In addition to donating money to fund-raising drives, he helped the school with its construction projects, lending building materials and even a work crew now and then when a new wing had to be added. So the question of disciplining Donald was one that had to be handled delicately; Fred Trump was too valuable an asset to risk alienating him.

Fred, however, turned out to be a cooperative parent. While he had to admire young Donald's energy and drive—indeed, recognized it as a genetic gift from himself—he also felt that it had to be channeled in the proper direction. Self-discipline was an important part of a successful man's makeup; without it a gifted individual with power and money behind him could develop into a monster. Donald, at this stage, was walking a narrow line separating youthful exuberance on one side and brattiness on the other. The boy had to be reined in.

Easier thought than done. All it took with Freddie was a disapproving look from his father. Donald was not so easily intimidated. The more Fred scolded him and tried to keep him in line, the more Donald rebelled. He didn't seem to be afraid of anyone. Fred thought he detected a touch of his own father in his second son, a hint of the devil in him. The boy stood up to him instinctively, as though he were out to prove that he was just as tough as his father was. "I used to fight back all the time," Donald said to Marie Brenner of *New York Magazine,* "My father was one tough son-of-a-gun. My father respects me because I stood up to him."

Donald's antics in school continued. He was a bright kid who did well in most of his subjects, but he enjoyed squirting soda at the girls, throwing birthday cakes at parties, and flinging erasers at teachers much more than he enjoyed studying for his exams.

7

Donald's closest buddy during these early school years was his brother Robert, two years his junior. Freddie was almost eight years older, too remote in age and temperament for Donald to have much in common with him. Rather than looking up to Freddie as an older brother, Donald perhaps viewed him as an interloper of sorts, a pretender to their father's throne, which Donald already considered rightfully his own. Freddie was someone to compete with. Maryanne, a full nine years older than Donald, was more of a surrogate mother than a sister. She was smart, tough, and just as determined as he was to make her own mark in life. Elizabeth was different. Not as bright as Maryanne or Donald, she made an easy target for his pranks and practical jokes. She did not lose her temper easily, but Donald had the ability to torment her to a level of fury. As far as she was concerned, he would always be "the brat" no matter how rich or famous he became later on.

Robert was Donald's natural ally, two grades behind him at the same school, the friend and brother whom he could tease playfully without causing hard feelings between them. As far as Robert was concerned, Donald was the perfect older brother, someone he could look up to and admire and who served as a buffer against the demands of their father. Robert was the more easy-going of the two; he felt no great mission to go out and set the world on fire, no sense of rivalry with his older brothers, no need to prove he was smarter and better than they were. When they were kids and Donald glued Robert's building blocks together, perhaps so that he could not build a structure taller than Donald's, Robert regarded it as just Donald being Donald and did not get upset about it. He deferred to Donald and was content to follow his lead. Not surprisingly they developed a warm affection for each other.

With all the overdriven energy and ambition that had already begun to show itself during his elementary school years, it was inevitable that Donald would turn to sports as an outlet. Union Turnpike, the bustling thoroughfare that connects Forest Hills and Jamaica Estates, is generously endowed with athletic fields for every season. The air is filled with the shouts of teenagers locked in combat in assorted competitions. It was to these arenas that Donald would gravitate after school, testing himself at football, baseball, soccer, and field hockey, depending on the time of year. Donald was, in fact, a natural athlete but physically on the slight side to be dominant on the football field (ownership of the New Jersey Generals would provide later compensation). Baseball was the sport he liked best, particularly stepping up to bat and smacking the hard white ball with all the leverage he could manage.

"It's not just strength, it's leverage. Even a small guy can hit a home run if he uses the right leverage," his baseball coach used to tell him. He didn't forget it, then or later.

Donald remained a hyper kid despite his extracurricular activities.

His energy seemed boundless, his enthusiasms unrestrained. It was almost as though he could not wait for his childhood years to end so that he could get on with the real business of life.

A rambunctious, defiant Donald was not the only problem Fred Trump was experiencing at this time. In September of 1954 Herbert Brownell, Jr., the Attorney General of the United States, formed a special grand jury, according to *The New York Times* on September 21, to investigate "bribery and other criminal conduct" in the housing business. The FBI had come up with evidence that Clyde L. Powell, the former assistant commissioner of the FHA, had provided windfalls totaling more than $51 million to home builders in 285 separate instances According to the FBI report, the FHA would grant loans that exceeded actual construction costs to various builders; the difference would be pocketed by the builders, and Powell would receive kickbacks as his end of the bargain. Over the years he had apparently received over $100,000 from his favored developers. Senator Homer Capehart, Republican of Indiana, lost no time in denouncing the scandal as even bigger than Teapot Dome, and used the term "windfall profits" to describe the affair.

Among the names that surfaced was Fred Trump. Fred admitted it was true that he had borrowed $10,398,600 from the FHA to build Shore Haven, and had actually put up the nine six-story structures for only $9,541,928 without accounting for the $856,672 difference. But he said that this was only made possible because of the sharp decline in the building materials market, the fact that he did his own building and had no builder's fee, and that the job was done faster than anticipated. It was also true, said Fred during his testimony in Washington, D.C., that he borrowed more from the FHA than it cost him to build the Beach Haven Apartments in Brighton Beach. But he denied that he had personally pocketed from $3.5 to $4 million in illegal profits, and he accused the federal government of "doing untold damage to my standing and reputation."

41

The FHA charged that the three corporations that built Shore Haven paid Fred more than $1.6 million in dividends between December 1949 and September 1951. Any disbursements without prior FHA approval would violate Shore Haven's corporate charter. "How much of this sum was legally withdrawn from the corporation cannot be determined until their books are available for FHA audit," said FHA Commissioner Norman P. Mason. On July 29, 1955, the FHA, controlled now by a new regime in Washington, was directed to replace Trump with new management at Shore Haven.

Fred's troubles were not finished. Over the years he had assembled a 29-acre parcel at the Luna Park site in Coney Island with the intention of building a $23 million housing project financed by FHA loans. In December 1955 the FHA withheld its approval for the project. The city paid Fred $1.5 million for the property, including a $49,000 allowance for interest above his reported purchase price of $1,451,000. "It is good to know people," Fred had told his children as they were growing up. He said at this time, according to *The New York Times* of December 9, 1955, that he was on the FHA's "blacklist" now but expected to "be taken off it soon, maybe in a few weeks."

With all this going on, it was only natural that Donald's high jinks at the Kew Forest School were giving his father a special headache. Maryanne graduated from the school, but he took Donald out in 1959 after the seventh grade and sent him off to the New York Military Academy, where, as he put it, "They straightened him out."

For good measure he took Robert out of Kew Forest, too, and sent him to the St. Paul's School in Garden City. An extra exposure to religion, he reasoned, couldn't do Donald's worshipful brother any harm.

8

Cornwall-on-Hudson is a sleepy town on the west bank of the river fifty-five miles north of New York City. The Palisades rise high above the Hudson at this point, providing the traveler with a breathtaking view across the fast-flowing river into Putnam County on the other side. There would be nothing to distinguish the village from a dozen others sprinkled along the shoreline were it not for the fact that Cornwall-on-Hudson is the home of the New York Military Academy, a prep school for the offspring of the affluent.

NYMA, or "Neema" as it is referred to by local residents, encompasses 325 acres of rolling countryside a thousand yards west of the river. Appropriately enough, the academy overlooks the town from the highest vantage point in the area, and its exclusivity is enhanced by a high wall of trees that cordons it off from the surrounding community. NYMA has about it the look of an old Spanish fort with its tan stucco buildings embellished with castle turrets, riding stables off to the west side of the campus, and a sampling of well-polished cannons of ancient vintage surrounding the quad. On any given day of the school year the students can be seen striding erectly around the campus or marching in precision on the parade grounds in uniforms similar to those worn by the cadets at West Point a few miles further to the south.

Donald Trump's favorite uniform was the crisp whites of the NYMA baseball team. "D.T." (as he was nicknamed by the other cadets) was the academy's star first baseman, good enough both in the field and at the plate for him to have given serious thought about pursuing a professional baseball career. He was tall now at six-feet-one and had the natural grace of a born athlete.

"He was a graceful kid," Theodore Dobias, his coach, told the author, "and he loved to go for the long ball."

According to Tobias, hitting a home run gave Donald more pleasure than just about anything else. Ironically enough, for a boy who had been such a discipline problem in grade school, he did not mind NYMA at all. It appeared at first as though his unharnessed energy might not blend all that well with the sobriety of a military environment, but he made the transition with no apparent difficulty. At the Kew Forest School Donald's classmates were from reasonably well-off families, most of them a notch or more below his own economic standing. At NYMA he had a chance to hobnob with students whose families boasted borderline social distinction in addition to money, and he found that this elevation in stature may well have suited him just fine.

At age thirteen Donald John Trump was a slim, handsome youngster with wavy sandy-blondish hair and an All-American-Boy look about him. His teachers recognized in him the traits of a natural leader. He loved to laugh and was extremely popular with his classmates. At the same time, there was nothing frivolous about his cheerful nature. He wore his uniform well and earned high grades without exerting any obvious effort. At the end of his first year he was classified Honor

Cadet, an accolade awarded to those who maintain an 85 average or better. This was a distinction he achieved in the ninth, eleventh, and twelfth grades as well, and in no year did his average drop below 80 percent.

Social life for the cadets centered around the various girls' schools in the region. (Today NYMA admits its "fair quota" of female cadets, but in the late 1950s and early 1960s it was an all-male preserve.) Almost every weekend there would be a dance at one of the academy's sister schools, and it was at these affairs that Donald had his first rude awakening about life, learning that being the handsome athletic son of a prominent New York City real estate developer was not quite enough for most of the girls he met. Something called "breeding" and "social position" seemed to carry more cachet than did a father who got his hands dirty working for a living, no matter how much money he had.

"Donald was kind of a fringe member of the social crowd, sort of out of it," said a woman who knew him in his NYMA days. "I never went out with him, and I could kill myself today for it."

Donald was, however, enough of a hit with pretty girls from families more like his own to be voted NYMA's "Ladies Man" by his fellow cadets.

His father's troubles on the political front back home certainly were not helping him with his social ambitions. During the 1961 campaign for mayor of New York City, the state attorney general, Louis J. Lefkowitz, denounced a Brooklyn fund-raising luncheon for Mayor Robert Wagner as "the ultimate expression of immorality." It was "a corrupt political shakedown," said the attorney general during a campaign rally covered by *The New York Times* on October 1, 1961.

According to Lefkowitz, the luncheon that was held the previous Wednesday at Sakele's restaurant in Brooklyn elicited pledges exceeding $25,000 from forty-three builders and real estate developers who attended. He cited the presence of Fred Trump, who had already donated $2,500 to Wagner's reelection campaign and was the promoter of the $65 million Warbasse housing project in Coney Island. Lefkowitz said that Trump and other developers were profiting from projects built under Title I programs of the federal government. Under these programs, blighted areas were acquired, cleared out, and then sold to developers at a loss. Two-thirds of the loss was subsidized by the federal government, with the balance picked up by the taxpayers of New York City. Then, under the Mitchell-Lama Act, loans of up to 90 percent of the construction costs were granted to the builders at extremely low interest rates. As icing on the cake, the developers received tax abatements averaging 50 percent to construct the buildings. Fred Trump's Warbasse proposal, said Lefkowitz, had already been approved as a Title I project with tax abatements ranging from 43 to 62 percent spread out over twenty years.

Lefkowitz accused the Wagner campaign coordinators of distributing blank checks among the developers at the luncheon, then asking them to stand up and declare for how much they were going to fill them in. The implication seemed to be that the larger the contribution the more would be the plums forthcoming from a Wagner administration in the future.

"Scandals have become the hallmark of the present city regime," Lefkowitz said in his fiery campaign style, according to *The New York Times*, and Trump's Warbasse deal was "...the most blatant scandal of all the scandals of the Wagner administration."

Such rhetoric notwithstanding, Robert Wagner went on to beat Governor Nelson Rockefeller's political protégé in what was considered to be a battle with the governor for control of New York City. After Lefkowitz was defeated the subject of Fred Trump and the other developers was forgotten for the time being.

* * *

During his summer breaks, Donald returned to the mansion on Midland Parkway and commuted daily with his father to his office and headquarters at 600 Avenue Z. Even at this early age Donald impressed his father, who was now approaching sixty, with his quick mind and natural instinct for the business. Donald was at his father's side when Fred announced the start of a 3,800-unit apartment complex to be built on 40 acres in Coney Island. The project would be known as Trump Village, and it would contain seven twenty-three-story towers, five of them with cooperative apartments and two with rentals, at an estimated total cost of $70 million.

Donald virtually lived at the construction site when he was not attending classes at NYMA. He loved the look and smell of the gaping holes in the ground, the grind of heavy earth-moving machines as they grappled with boulders and tree stumps. No longer was there a doubt in anyone's mind who was Fred Trump's number-one son. Freddie was born too soon, out of turn as it were, and he carried his father's name only because of this accident of birth. But Donald was the natural heir, the one who was born to carry on and expand his father's work. Freddie, now in his early twenties, had already left home to pursue his own dreams while Donald could not wait to finish school and do the work he was destined for. There was never any conscious decision made by either father or son. Donald's path would be a continuation of the one laid down by Fred Trump forty years before. No decision was necessary; it seemed genetically ordained.

Donald returned to NYMA, the academy along the Hudson River, and took his place in the graduation class of 1964. His record was distinguished if not spectacular. He was an Honor Cadet for four of the five years he attended, and a Proficient Cadet the other year. In addition, he had performed well on the football field in 1962, on the soccer field in 1963, and well enough on the baseball diamond from 1962 through 1964 to receive the Coach's Award in that sport. He was

47

expected to attend college before going to work full time with his father, and the college he selected was Fordham University, the Jesuit institution on the green, tree-filled campus in the northern section of the Bronx.

Part Two

THE YOUNG BARON

9

It did not take Donald Trump long to realize that the Jesuits at Fordham University and he had embarked upon a serious collision course. After five years of uniforms and parades at NYMA he evidently felt a need for a change of pace and the militaristic Jesuits were not the answer. During the previous few years he and his father had grown closer than ever, and even at eighteen Donald had learned a good deal about real estate and was itching to put the books behind him and start working full time in the family business. But Fred insisted that he get a degree, something he himself had never accomplished. If nothing else, a piece of paper would give him more credibility later on. The undergraduate business school at Wharton on the University of Pennsylvania campus was reputed to have one of the best real estate programs in the country. Donald agreed to transfer from Fordham to Wharton during his first year, and bide his time a bit longer before pursuing his career.

By this time his sister Maryanne had gotten her law degree from Rutgers and was practicing in New Jersey. She was married to a Newark attorney named John J. Barry, and it was evident that her goal of becoming successful on her own was already being realized. Young Fred's story was different. He had left home with no sense of direction except to be away from his father's influence. He talked about doing many things but followed through on nothing. Depression seemed to follow wherever he went and he quickly became discouraged at whatever he tried. There were also rumors about his heavy drinking. Along the way he acquired a girl friend named Linda, a petite and attractive brunette, and they were talking about getting married. With no great sense of mission, more because he did not know what else he wanted to do, he learned to fly and applied for a job as a pilot with TWA. The younger daughter, Elizabeth, had never been a great mystery to anyone. Friendly and outgoing, she did not have any burning ambition to be a great achiever and went to work as a secretary for the Chase Manhattan Bank in Manhattan. Robert was still in high school, and Donald missed him and their good times together more than anything else.

Donald agreed to attend Wharton for his father's sake. He showed up for classes and did what was required of him but he was clearly bored and spent a lot of time on outside business activites. Like his father, Donald was a teetotaler and a nonsmoker. It was not a moral question; he just could never see the sense of altering his perception or sucking smoke into his lungs. He looked a bit like Ed "Kooky" Byrnes, a teenage idol of the day, with his high blondish pompadour. His taste in clothing was a trifle on the flashy side, running to burgundy suits and matching suede shoes. Despite his, literally, sober nature, he had developed a cockiness in his attitudes—some called it youthful brashness and others called it arrogance—that was tempered by a keen sense of humor, even if it tended on occasion to be a bit condescending.

If there was one individual other than his father whom Donald held in great esteem it was the flamboyant real estate developer, William Zeckendorf. To be sure, he admired Zeckendorf's great accomplishments as a master builder, but what he idolized most about the man was his style. Zeckendorf knew how to get attention. He was the Mike Todd of the real estate world, a showman as well as a businessman, his own best promoter and publicity agent. There was no way that Zeckendorf would sit anonymously on a stage while some windbag of a bureaucrat neglected to mention his name. Zeckendorf's style, his persona, was an integral part of everything he built. His work was a kind of existential statement: I build, therefore I am. Donald hero-worshiped the legendary developer and considered him a role model.

At the same time Donald was learning more from his father than how to put up buildings. He was getting a firsthand education on how to roll with the punches when the going got rough. While Donald was marking time at Wharton, coasting through courses he could have been teaching himself, Fred was embroiled in another controversy at home. This one involved the first project to bear his name: Trump Village in Brooklyn. The seven twenty-three-story towers were built over a period of several years with 90 percent financing from the state. Fred received the 7.25 percent builder's profit allowed by law, but according to Leo E. Silverman, a state auditor testifying before the New York State Investigation Commission, it was based on an estimated cost that was $6,650,000 higher than the actual construction cost. This resulted in a windfall of $598,000, plus an additional $1,228,000 in profits from the purchase of the 40 acres of land at a lower cost than he originally claimed. As a result, according to Silverman, Fred Trump had taken in $1,825,000 more than he was entitled to.

"Is there any way to prevent a man who does business like that from getting another contract with the state?" asked state investigator Jacob Grumet during a hearing in January 1966, reported in *The New York Times* on January 27.

"I don't think so, under our present laws," answered Silverman.

Fred was also criticized for his employment of Abraham M. Lindenbaum, a former member of the New York City Planning Commission, as his lawyer in acquiring the building site. Through Lindenbaum's efforts, Fred had prevented another builder from developing the land over a period of three years until he was able to develop it himself. For his labors, Lindenbaum then billed New York State for $520,000 in legal fees. In effect, one might say that the taxpayers of the state were being asked to pay Fred Trump's legal fees. Another of Fred's attorneys, MacNeil Mitchell, sent the state a $128,000 bill for his services in selling the cooperative apartments at Trump Village.

Mr. Lindenbaum had originally been appointed to the City Planning Commission in July 1960 by Mayor Robert F. Wagner. He resigned his post in September 1961 when Louis Lefkowitz revealed him to be the impresario of the controversial fund-raising luncheon at Sakele's restaurant that the Attorney General objected to during the mayoral campaign that year.

What did Mr. Lindenbaum do to earn a $520,000 legal fee? Apparently he had worked to condemn the land and to evict the existing tenants from the blighted area so that his client could build Trump Village on the site. Since there were a thousand tenants living there at the time, the going rate for getting rid of unwanted tenants was evidently $520 apiece. It was not said in so many words, but the implication was that the taxpayers of the state had received good value for their money: another lawyer, after all, might have charged $1,000 a tenant. At these proceedings it appeared that Fred Trump may have charged the state heavily for construction equipment leased by a firm that he himself owned.

Was this true? the state investigator wanted to know. Did he really overcharge for leasing equipment he owned?

"I've got forty-three corporations I'm sole stock owner in," said Fred, according to the same report, "and these things escape my mind sometimes."

The incident, which provided Donald with a far more practical education than he was getting in college, remained under investigation for six years before it surfaced again. As will be seen, it was eventually resolved to Fred's satisfaction.

10

Meanwhile, bored at Wharton, Donald attended classes because he had to in order to get his degree, but he spent his time off-campus as much as possible. He joined no clubs or fraternities and did not participate in campus political organizations. His baseball career was likewise laid to rest. It would seem that, like most everything else in his life, if he could not be the best, a major leaguer, he would not play at all.

To keep in practice more than anything else, he bought and renovated several properties in Philadelphia during his undergraduate years, experience he felt of more value than the classroom theorizing of his professors. On his summer vacations he worked with his father in the Brooklyn office, helping Fred negotiate a number of deals while he continued to learn the business. He was already thinking ahead, planning projects far more adventuresome than anything his father had

built. Donald Trump had bigger things in mind than putting up yet
another row of two-family houses in Brooklyn or Queens.

"Donald always used to talk about changing the Manhattan skyline,"
said a college friend of his, reflecting back on their Wharton days.

He also learned a good deal from the unexpected problems that came
down on his idol, William Zeckendorf, during the mid-1960s. Zeckendorf, the flamboyant showman, was suddenly on the verge of bankruptcy after a career filled with kingly wealth and worldwide fame.
His organization hemorrhaging money, he was obliged to sell off the
outposts of his empire at bargain basement prices to raise cash. A 500-
acre parcel in downtown Toronto was auctioned off to the Reichman
brothers of Olympia & York for $17.8 million, perhaps a third of its
true market value. The land was later developed into First Canadian
Place, the seventy-two-story flagship of the Reichman empire and the
hub of the fastest-growing city in North America during the next
decade. Donald analyzed Zeckendorf's troubles, and vowed never to
make the same mistakes himself.

Zeckendorf ignored the three golden rules of real estate: "Location,
location, location," Donald reflected several years afterward. "If you
go to Paris, if you go to Duluth, the best location is called the Tiffany
location. That is a standard real estate phrase."

In addition, William Zeckendorf had allowed his basic business
sense to become clouded by his own mythology, his belief that he
could do no wrong.

"Zeckendorf remembered to multiply, but he forgot to add," Donald
stated. What he meant was that during times of economic hardship
one wants to be a buyer of land at depressed prices, not a landlord
with vacant offices to rent. Zeckendorf had fallen into the trap of
putting up luxury buildings, financed at high interest rates when the
economy was booming, and then having to rent them out when a
recession hit and everybody was strapped for cash. The Reichmans
knew, and Donald was learning, that a recession offers an opportunity

to buy at low prices. and that the ensuing boom is the time to lease out space or sell property when prices are rising. Buy and build when things look bleak; lease and sell when the economy hits a peak.

Donald said that he used these years at Wharton to sort out his ideas and firm up his plans. He also has said he even thought briefly about going into the oil business instead of pursuing a real estate career. It is difficult to believe that he ever gave *serious* thought about doing anything other than what he seemed born to do: surpass his father and the other real estate barons by building the most talked-about buildings of our time.

When he graduated from Wharton in May 1968, he did not stay around long enough to have his picture taken with his class. It has been reported that he graduated first in the class, but Donald denied that he ever made such a claim. Actually he was not among the honor students that year.

Donald's return to the family home in Jamaica Estates could not have come at a more propitious time so far as his father was concerned; not that Fred was slowing down at the age of sixty-two. He still put in marathon ten- and twelve-hour workdays in his Brooklyn office, often working six days a week. But Fred was experiencing one of the first major setbacks of his long career, and Donald's arrival on the scene helped alleviate some of the strain.

Fred Trump's problem concerned the 12.5-acre site of the old Steeplechase Park in Coney Island. At one time Steeplechase Park had been a popular amusement center, its thirty-two rides attracting people from every borough of New York City as well as tourists from out of town. But it had fallen on hard times and was now losing money, largely because of the rundown condition of the surrounding neighborhood. When the park finally closed Fred Trump acquired it from the daughter of George Tilyou, the deceased owner, for $2.5 million. Steeplechase was located between the boardwalk and Surf Avenue, stretching from West 16th to West 19th streets. Fred planned to build what he described as "a modern Miami Beach high-rise apartment dwelling" on the site, with balconies facing the beach overlooking the Atlantic Ocean.

But August Heckscher, New York City's parks commissioner, had other ideas. There was a new administration in City Hall—John Vliet Lindsay, a reform-minded Republican, had replaced Robert Wagner as mayor in 1966. Lindsay had trounced Fred Trump's own favorite candidate, Abraham Beame of the Brooklyn Democratic organization, in the 1965 election. Fred did not have the same influence with the Lindsay people that he had with the Brooklyn Democrats. Heckscher, a Lindsay appointee, reasoned that Steeplechase Park, which was opened in 1897, was now a city landmark and should remain zoned for recreational use.

Fred tried to salvage his proposal by revising it from a "Miami Beach high-rise" to a middle-income housing development for the elderly. He would build four thirty-story apartment buildings with 3,000 units, he said, for $60 million. Financing for the project would be through low-interest loans under the Mitchell-Lama Law, coupled with a 50 percent tax abatement. He could house ten thousand elderly people, he said, at a cost of $28 a room per month. The city, however, remained firm in its opposition to rezoning the area for residential use. As commendable as Fred Trump's plans were to provide additional housing for the elderly, the public, the city said, would be best served by creating a new seafront park on the site. Alfred Shapiro, a spokesman for August Heckscher, declared:

"The city has a vision of building a combination Disneyland and Tivoli Gardens." He envisioned a monumental park with indoor swimming pools, restaurants, and concert facilities. "We'll build things on top of things," he said grandly, with a multilevel seafront park development.

Fred Trump listened patiently to Mr. Shapiro's visions, then replied that his plan would save the taxpayers of New York City $15 million in land acquisition and improvement costs, plus $1 million a year in debt service. Even with his 50 percent tax abatement, he added, he would still be contributing $1 million a year to the city in real estate taxes. To complicate matters further, a meeting was held at the New School for Social Research to discuss the matter of public housing. Several spokesmen maintained that the city should build low-income housing for the poor and that housing should be treated as just another public utility. Alfred Shapiro, somewhat perplexed that the needy, whose interests were foremost in his mind, had turned up their noses at his multilevel recreational paradise, declared that the city could not afford to spend the "tens of millions of dollars" required to build such a project.

In the end there was the not unusual breakdown of winners and losers. On May 23, 1968, the very day that young Donald was exiting quick-time from the Wharton campus, the Board of Estimate ruled that the 12.5-acre Steeplechase Park site would be retained for recreational use. It directed the city to apply immediately to the federal government for a $2 million grant to build a park.

Fred Trump received $4 million from the city for the land, a sum that represented a 60 percent return on investment over the three years he held it. It was a handsome profit by any standard. The poor were denied a publicly financed housing project and would be treated instead to an oceanside fun palace, a place to frolic not too far from the existing tenements in the area. And the taxpayers were asked to pick up the tab for yet another pipedream, this one spun from the brain of August Heckscher, the would-be Robert Moses of the Lindsay administration.

It is worth noting that in 1984, sixteen years after this episode, the old Steeplechase Park site remained exactly that—an open stretch of rubble-strewn land not being utilized for anything. As the French say, *plus ça change, plus c'est la même chose*, the more things change, the more they are the same.

City dreamers, yes. Donald Trump, no.

11

Donald John Trump was now in his element. His first job after embarking upon a full-time participation in the Trump organization was to take a careful look at his father's books. He was immediately struck by the amount of equity buildup in the various projects Fred had constructed over the years. His father had always been a cautious man, not borrowing too heavily when he had to pay the going bank rate and using as much leverage as possible when low-interest government loans were available. Over the decades the houses and apartment buildings Fred put up had appreciated dramatically, and Donald asked his father to refinance the properties to free up the tens of millions of dollars that lay dormant in them. In many cases mortgages had been paid down completely, and the buildings could be refinanced at 90 to 100 percent of their market value.

Fred apparently was hesitant at first, cautious about taking on a mountain of debt that would have to be regularly serviced. But Donald's enthusiasm won him over. According to real estate people the author spoke to, Donald evidently convinced his father that cash flow from the rents would more than pay the interest charges. If the worst happened and depression struck, they would already have their money out of the properties and would not have to worry about collapsing real estate values. Let the banks seize the buildings and auction them off to the highest bidder. Their money was out. It was a smart financial move.

Donald had other dreams besides just raising cash for money's sake alone. He already had his vision fixed on Manhattan, the glittering borough just across the East River. He knew that, successful as his father had been during the previous forty-five years, true recognition depended on making it in Manhattan. By taking cash out of their properties in the outer boroughs, the Trumps could use it to pyramid their fortune into a full-scale empire. At age twenty-two the young baron's dreams had already begun to assume the dimensions of empire.

But Fred drew the line. He went along with his son's refinancing notions, but every time Donald tried to tug him westward toward Manhattan, Fred trotted him over to the Oranges in New Jersey to look at a site for a housing project for the aged, to Las Vegas to check out apartment complexes, and as far south as Florida to build some genuine Miami Beach high-rises in their natural habitat. Fred still had dreams of expanding his barony as much as his son did; he just felt more comfortable doing it on familiar turf.

Still, except for his ambition to invade the Big Apple, Donald was given his head and he was grateful for it.

"I gave Donald free rein," Fred said in an interview years later. "He has great vision and everything he touches seems to turn to gold. As long as he has this great energy in abundance, I'm glad to let him do it. Donald is the smartest person I know," he added proudly.

The Trump barony continued to grow with new vigor, primarily because of Donald's unbounded enthusiasms. If he could not convince his father to challenge the Manhattan empires of Harry Helmsley, the Durst Organization, Rudin Management, the Fisher brothers, Preston Robert Tisch, and Sylvan Lawrence, at least he would get the old man out of the boroughs. But housing projects for the aged in New Jersey, however worthy, were hardly the sort of projects Donald had in mind.

Father and son now journeyed west to California to buy land, down to Maryland, Virginia, and Washington, D.C. to put up apartment buildings, and most frequently to Florida, where Fred could indulge his lifelong infatuation with Miami Beach high-rises. When they were home together in New York, they commuted from Jamaica Estates to Coney Island each day in Fred's chauffeur-driven limousine with the letters "FT" on the license plates. Visitors to the unpretentious Trump organization headquarters located in the rear of a middle-income apartment building never failed to notice the incongruous limousine parked beside the building.

"Who owns that?" they might ask, wondering if royalty had inexplicably descended upon the neighborhood. When the managers of the East Orange housing project stopped by one day to drop off some rent checks, they walked past the limousine, studied it in wonderment, then entered the somewhat dingy office with cigar store Indians propped against the walls. The surroundings looked as though they belonged to any one of a dozen landlords they knew who owned perhaps two or three buildings in New Jersey. Fred greeted them politely, then disappeared into a back office while a tall, lanky boy in a maroon suit came out to see them.

"Who owns that limousine outside?" asked Ivan Shore, the younger of the two visitors, a young man no older than Donald whom I interviewed in 1984.

"We do. Why?"

The visitors looked at each other. Things were not what they appeared to be.

63

"My father and I own twenty-four thousand units in New York City," said Donald with a mischievous smile on the corner of his lips as he accepted the checks from them.

The managing agents nearly swooned. The owner of fifty or sixty units was a big man where they came from; a hundred to two hundred units was awe-inspiring. But twenty-four *thousand* units! These people were sultans.

"We're building mostly in Florida now," Donald continued briskly, but the men hardly heard a word he said. All they knew, all that impressed them at the moment, was that they were sitting in the presence of more money than they ever imagined existed.

12

Donald was still determined to make his mark in Manhattan, one way or another. If his father refused to enter the high-stakes world of major league real estate, Donald could at least set up a campaign headquarters there from which he could better observe the battlefield. He moved into a bachelor's apartment (which he would describe as a three-bedroom penthouse apartment) in the brown-brick and concrete Phoenix Building at 160 East 65th Street, a regal spread suitable for a young baron on his way to becoming a superbaron.

His tastes were already established by this time. His notion of appropriate business attire included burgundy suits with matching patent leather shoes. His initials were sewn into his shirts in matching-colored threads and were likewise engraved on his gold cuff links. He commuted from his apartment to the Brooklyn office each day in a silver chauffeur-driven Cadillac limousine with "DJT" on the license plates.

Now there were two limos parked outside the office with the cigar store Indians in Coney Island—FT's and DJT's, enough to overwhelm any visiting rental agents from across the Hudson River.

If Fred's taste ran to towering apartment buildings with V-shaped balconies overlooking the ocean, Donald added to it with a touch of Beverly Hills, an extra dimension acquired during his frequent sorties to the West Coast. To the glitter-glass and aquamarine tile that characterized Fred's buildings, Donald contributed doses of chrome, quartz, and marble. He had already moved beyond pastel apartments with goldfish swimming in the lobbies. He decorated his own apartment in beige and brown velvet with adornments of chrome and crystal. Some guests at the time said it looked more like a movie set than a residence, but one must never underestimate the little green men. When he invited his friend Der Scutt, a New York architect, over to help him decorate, the man was surely surprised:

"When I got to his penthouse apartment in that brick building across from the Sign of the Dove, I looked at this stuff, velvet and chrome, Donald had purchased on Third Avenue, and I just pushed most of it in the hall and arranged the rest." Scutt recalled the incident for me with affection. Donald, not yet twenty-four, was developing a style all his own.

Donald's social life was active, bringing him in close contact with jet-setters and other trendy on-the-make New Yorkers in places such as El Morocco, Regine's, Le Club, and Doubles. Still a teetotaler and a nonsmoker, he had an appreciative eye for the stewardesses, as they were then still called, and fashion models who frequented these establishments looking to meet rich availables like Donald Trump. He took his dates to "21" for dinner, enjoying the scene of famous actors, sports figures, politicians, and other celebrities who ate and drank there. (One day people would go to "21" to look at him.) When he was not partying at the eastside clubs or dining at his favorite restaurant, he enjoyed taking in the Knicks and Rangers games at Madison Square Garden, where he had season tickets.

When his father asked him if he was getting serious about any of his girl friends, Donald replied, "Their heads are all screwed on wrong."

Donald even at this early stage of his life already had well-developed theories about people with "elan," "flair," and "style." He admired people who possessed those traits, and frankly numbered himself among them. They were "the very best people," and they were the ones he would especially like to build for.

"If a man has flair," he said, "and is smart and somewhat conservative and has a taste for what people want, he's bound to be successful in New York." One also needed drive and singlemindedness, which Donald himself had in abundance.

When Donald was made president of the Trump organization, his position as the heir apparent to his father's position became official. The second son of Fred Trump, not his firstborn son and namesake, would rule the kingdom. Freddie had walked away from the battlefield and, therefore, away from any claim to the role. But his displacement by the kid brother who was everything his father hoped he would be still hurt. Freddie's already fragile psyche was tipped a bit further, said a family associate to the author. In his flight from the Trump barony he married Linda, the attractive woman he had been seeing, and they had two children. They named the boy Frederick Charles after his father and the girl Mary after his mother. Freddie went to work as a pilot for TWA, but almost from the start there was a question of how long he could continue. Freddie reportedly had a history of drinking.

Maryanne and her lawyer husband, John J. Barry, were busy raising a family of their own in New Jersey. She was on the verge of being appointed to a seat on the federal bench, based in the Federal Building in Trenton, while her husband practiced law in Newark. Elizabeth still worked as a secretary for the Chase Manhattan Bank, where the Trumps did much of their banking. And Robert, the youngest, was finishing college. Well over six feet now, as tall as Donald and somewhat more beefy, he emulated his older brother as much as he could, and planned to follow his footsteps into the family business.

So the line was from the patriarch to the second son to the last. Trump, no trump, double Trump.

13

The Winter Olympics opened in Sapporo, Japan, on February 3, 1972. Emperor Hirohito presided over a banquet welcoming 1,125 athletes from thirty-five different nations, a turnout second only to the 1,293 who competed in Grenoble, France, in 1968.

One of the alternates on the Czechoslovakian downhill skiing team was a tall blond woman with the looks and figure of a fashion model. Born in Vienna, raised mostly in Czechoslovakia, her mother's home country, she learned to ski when she was a small girl and loved the thrill of speed whether from downhill racing or in a speedboat flying at open throttle across a lake. She badly wanted to win a medal at Sapporo but never got the chance to compete. Throughout the competition she sat on the sidelines and looked on in frustration as Marie Therese Nadig of Switzerland won the women's downhill, beating the odds-on favorite, Annemarie Proell of Austria. The skier's name was Ivana Zelnickova Winklmayr.

Never mind. Ivana presumably had better things in mind than being just another Olympic skier whose name would be forgotten a week after the games were over. It may not have been certain how she would manage it, but she evidently decided to go to America and become somebody truly important.

In New York City Donald Trump, the man Ivana Winklmayr would eventually link her destiny to, was also working on stardom. At the moment, though, the kind of attention the Trump name was attracting created a different sort of image than the one desired. Donald had visions of soaring Manhattan skyscrapers, if possible named after himself, ultramodern marvels of architectural accomplishment. Instead, his father's deals seemed to be conjuring images of smoke-filled rooms and kept politicians.

In the headlines were stories of alleged payoffs from the construction industry to city housing inspectors and other public officials amounting to over $25 million a year. "Hardly a stove is moved in New York City without someone getting paid under the table for it," claimed Robert K. Ruskin, the city's investigation commissioner, who estimated that between one and two percent of total construction costs were earmarked for officials who overlooked violations of building and safety regulations. In this atmosphere three government agencies moved to block the payment of the $520,000 bill Abraham Lindenbaum submitted for the work he performed as Fred Trump's attorney. The State Commission of Investigation, the City Investigation Department, and the Corporation Counsel claimed that the drawing up of a list of tenants slated for eviction from the Trump Village site, plus the dispersement of eviction notices, had been done by New York City's Corporation Counsel, not Mr. Lindenbaum.

"I worked on that job for seven years, from 1959 to 1965," replied an irate Lindenbaum, as reported by *The New York Times* of October 10, 1972.

"It certainly was a well-earned fee," Fred Trump concurred. "He handled the negotiations and drew up the contracts." He noted that the $520,000 fee would be passed along to the tenants and would cost each apartment only $125. "I think that speaks for itself."

Bernard Botein, a former presiding justice of the Appellate Division, was asked to remove himself as the arbitrator in the dispute on the grounds that he had been retained as an attorney by Lindenbaum. Apparently Lindenbaum had hired Botein in a 1970 rent stabilization case and allegedly paid him $100,000 for his services. Botein acknowledged that this was true (except to say that the amount was "well under $100,000") but that it made no difference:

"It would not affect my judgment," he said. In any event, he continued, he had not wanted to take the case in the first place but had been urged to do so by both Lindenbaum and the city. Evidently he was desired by all parties involved. He was doing his duty.

The case dragged on for several months. Eventually it came to pass that Abraham Lindenbaum was paid his fee, Botein maintained his relationship with the city and Lindenbaum, and the tenants paid a bit extra to defray the costs. The way of the world—or at least the world of politics, real estate, and accommodation in the City of New York.

71

14

By the beginning of 1973, fifty years after Fred Trump built his first house in the Woodhaven section of Queens, Trump properties in New York were valued at an estimated $150 million while out-of-town Trump holdings amounted to approximately $50 million. Fred Trump, now sixty-seven years of age, had built thousands of one- and two-family houses during his long career, and he and his son owned dozens of apartment complexes under a network of fifty-eight separate corporations. The rent rolls from their apartments in New York City alone came to more than $50 million a year. By Donald's calculations, the aggregate worth of the Trump organization had grown from $40 million to $200 million during the five years he had been working full time with his father. A 500 percent increase.

It was inevitable that a young man as ambitious and intelligent as Donald Trump would sooner or later have his way. On the occasion of Fred's fiftieth anniversary as a builder, father and son announced together that they were entering the dynamic Manhattan real estate market. The kid demonstrably had a golden touch, and Fred reluctantly agreed to go along with his plans to invade the territory on the other side of the East River. They had recently acquired a site on the eastside of Manhattan, the Trumps announced, on which they planned to put up an apartment building. The area was in the East 60s, not too far from Donald's penthouse apartment. The units would be strictly for rental. "We are not interested in converting to cooperatives," Fred said in an attempt to defuse the growing criticism that real estate developers were destroying the country's supply of rental housing by converting everything to cooperatives and condominiums.

Fred Trump was still tall and slim at sixty-seven, with a full head of dark graying hair, handsome in a 1940s movie-star way, sporting a swept-back pompadour and a dark pencil-line mustache. Indeed, he looked as though he might have stepped out of an old movie starring Barbara Stanwyck or Joan Crawford—the mysterious charmer, faintly dangerous. Donald, as tall as Fred (both men standing a couple of inches over six feet), handsome, clean-shaven—with only a hint of a pouty sneer at times crossing his lips. He wore his hair longer now than at NYMA and Wharton, in a sort of Robert Redford windblown style. He kept in shape with vigorous games of tennis, squash, and racquetball as often as he could fit them into his busy schedule, and he played a good game of golf when he had the time to get out on the course on weekends.

In getting his way with his father on the Manhattan land arrangement, Donald was following the advice he had given to his friend Richard Lefrak, the son of Samuel Lefrak of Lefrak City. The elder Lefrak was a hard-working, self-made man from the old school, just as Fred was, the kind who could overwhelm a son with the power of his energy and personality without even realizing it.

"Don't let Sam run over you," Donald told Richard repeatedly. "Get out from under his thumb. My father respects me because I stood up to him. You have to show some guts."

There was no question that Fred respected and admired his second-born son more than perhaps anyone else. Donald at only twenty-six was smarter and more capable than anyone else Fred had dealt with, and he was not reluctant to say so. His decision to let Donald have his way on the Manhattan transaction marked the beginning of the shift in power from father to son in the Trump organization. Fred was not yet ready to step aside completely and cede control to Donald; he knew he never would be. He was not the sort to retire and spend his days on a Florida golf course as long as he had the ability to put in a full day's work. But he knew instinctively that Donald was right, that the future of the Trump barony—if it were to continue to grow and expand to the dimensions of empire—depended on their engaging the Manhattan real estate titans successfully in their own theater of operation. Donald's course was the only logical one for them to take. Anything less would be a diversion, a cop-out, a refusal to participate in the high-stakes game of major league real estate. Besides, Fred was not one to duck a fight.

If they were going to compete successfully, the Trumps would have to reestablish their ties with City Hall. John Lindsay, the Golden Boy from New York's Silk Stocking district, had cold-shouldered them for the previous eight years. Lindsay had announced he would not run for reelection as mayor of New York City in 1973, which left the field open for a reliable Brooklyn organization Democrat to step in and recapture the office.

Abraham Beame, a diminutive accountant from Brooklyn, wanted to make another try for the mayoralty. Fred urged Abe to run. He had been to the Jamaica Estates home for dinner, and the Trumps had made campaign contributions. Not unreasonably, they hoped that perhaps one day Abe Beame would ascend to a position of real power in the

74

city. Having lost in 1965 to Lindsay, Beame was now anxious to give the mayoralty race a second try. And perhaps as much as anyone else, except the once-defeated candidate, Fred Trump, and son Donald, wanted Abraham Beame to be the next mayor of New York City.

15

Abraham David Beame was born in London on March 20, 1906. His parents, Polish refugees from poverty and persecution, worked for a while in London until the way was clear for them to emigrate to the United States. Young Abe attended public schools in New York City and shortly after finishing college in 1928 married his long-time friend, Mary Ingerman.

The newlyweds moved to an apartment not too far from Prospect Park in Brooklyn. Almost immediately Beame joined the Madison Club in the same borough, the headquarters of the powerful Democratic organization that had turned out so many of the city's more influential politicians since the early days of the century. Slowly Abe Beame worked his way up through the city's bureaucracy, serving in various appointed positions in different administrations, and with a degree in accounting was finally elected comptroller of New York City on the

Wagner ticket in 1961. Four years later the Brooklyn organization persuaded him to run for mayor against a tall, handsome, charismatic Republican named John V. Lindsay. Lindsay was the "Golden Boy," a smiling, stretched-out version of Paul Newman. On a note of comic relief, the Conservative Party nominated William F. Buckley, Jr. as its candidate. Buckley lost no time in announcing that if by some quirk of fate he happened to win the race he would demand a recount. Whatever the relative merits, the placid, five-foot-two-inch Abe Beame, sandwiched between the acerbic Buckley on one side and the six-foot-four-inch movie-star-handsome Lindsay on the other side, was, cosmetically at least, out of his depth.

To make their candidate more viable, the Democratic Party undertook to refurbish his personality, or at least his persona. A nice man, a decent man, a normally self-effacing man, he was told to come out slugging, to abandon his Mr. Nice Guy nature and slam Lindsay. The role did not come easily to Abe Beame; it did not suit him at all. And of course he lost. After the election Beame reverted to his normal self and acknowledged with characteristic candor:

"I wanted to start off by saying I'm not as glib as Mr. Lindsay, not as ready with a quick capsule answer. But what does that have to do with being mayor? That's what I wanted to say, but they wouldn't let me."

By "they" he meant the party leaders back in Brooklyn. But it was too late. The election was lost. And Fred Trump was not happy. He had donated handsomely to Beame's campaign, and was not accustomed to backing losers. It might be said, to paraphrase Lyndon Johnson when he commented on George Romney's quest for the presidency a few years later, watching Abraham Beame running for mayor in a manner that was against his better instincts was like watching a duck trying to fuck a football. But Abe Beame did manage to rehabilitate himself considerably in 1969 when he was once again elected comptroller, ironically in a race that saw Lindsay win reelection as mayor.

But now it was 1973 and things were different. The voters' infatuation with the Golden Boy had dissolved into thin air. New York was flirting with bankruptcy, and Lindsay, rightly or wrongly, was blamed for most of the problems. The mood of the electorate had changed. John Lindsay chose not to run again. The people were ready for someone safe, dependable, and *not* flamboyant or charismatic. Somebody who at least knew how to count, who understood such things as cash flow and deficit spending—an accountant, say, who did not entertain grandiose schemes that might push the city further over the cliff into financial oblivion. The time was now right for somebody not too glib, not too pretty, nor even witty. Somebody who did not stand out in a crowd. Somebody, indeed, like Abe Beame.

Abe and Mary Beame still lived in a three-room apartment just off Prospect Park, and in the summer rented a second-floor apartment in Belle Harbor, Queens, with a view of Long Island Sound and the Throgs Neck Bridge. How could one not love, or at least feel comfortable with, someone who wintered in Brooklyn and summered in Queens? The Beames' lifestyle was not dissimilar to that of a good-natured Archie Bunker. Saturday nights were usually spent playing gin rummy with neighbors or watching television. During the week Abe got home from work about seven o'clock and sat down with Mary for a light supper, usually a piece of melon, a salad, perhaps a plate of leftover chicken fricassee and a dish of ice cream. If they did not watch television in the time remaining before retiring, they played checkers by themselves or with a next-door neighbor.

"We never go out to movies or parties," Mary said with a smile during the campaign, "and our tastes definitely don't run to filet mignon. After all those roast beef political dinners, I don't care if I never see another piece of beef again."

If the people were looking for a dramatic change after eight years of controversial, provocative, combative, flamboyant John Lindsay, they could not have manufactured a more suitable alternative than

Abraham Beame. Running against him in his second try for the mayor's office were Republican John Marchi, a low-key professorial type who tended to philosophize over the issues rather than debate them; Conservative Mario Biaggi, a "law-and-order" congressman from the Bronx; and Liberal Albert Blumenthal, who turned out to be Beame's toughest critic in the campaign. The Liberals had broken with the Democratic Party in what amounted to an ugly family dispute. Actually they preferred John Lindsay, who had made an effort to expose what they considered corruption of earlier administrations, and regarded Beame as too much a part of the old party system with questionable ties to the real estate interests. Painting his argument with a broad brush, Blumenthal attacked Beame as a creature of "bossism," who was dominated by the real estate industry. So the battle lines were drawn.

Three weeks before the election a scandal erupted that threatened to have a serious impact on the New York mayoralty race. On the same day that Spiro Agnew held a press conference to announce that he had resigned the vice-presidency of the United States to help Richard Nixon "restore unimpaired confidence and implicit trust" to his administration, it was alleged by the Department of Justice that Trump Management Corporation was discriminating against blacks in the rental of apartments. In doing so, the government claimed, the corporation violated the Fair Housing Act of 1968. Donald Trump, president of the company, denied the charges:

"They are absolutely ridiculous. We never have discriminated and we never would. There have been a number of local actions against us and we've won them all. We proved in court that we did not discriminate."

Nor would the Trumps accept the same settlement that Samuel Lefrak did when he was accused of racial discrimination at Lefrak City. Samuel's son Richard, acting as a spokesman for his father, denied that they had discriminated but agreed to open up a percentage of their rental units to people on welfare. In return for this concession the government dropped its charges. But Donald Trump refused to capitulate to the Department of Justice. Of the 16,000 units in question, he said, more than 700 were at the time rented to blacks. Under no circumstances, though, would the Trumps rent apartments to anyone on welfare unless they had guaranteed income levels.

The only criterion was whether or not they could afford to pay the rent, and whether there would be a suitable number of tenants for the rooms. Renting to people on welfare would be unfair to the other tenants. It would lead to a "massive fleeing" of the neighborhood by everyone else, Donald has said. He decided to tough it out.

Notwithstanding headline-making charges about the real estate industry in general and the Trumps in particular, together with Blumenthal's attempts to link Abe Beame to the group, the voters refused to be swayed. On Tuesday, November 6, 1973, Abraham David Beame was elected the 104th mayor of New York City in a landslide victory. He rolled up a whopping 955,388 votes, nearly 60 percent of the total. Marchi came in an embarrassing second, barely beating Blumenthal, with 275,362 votes to the Liberal candidate's 263,604. Biaggi was fourth with 189,135 votes.

During the victory celebration at the Biltmore Hotel, Abe Beame strode to the podium to thank the six hundred supporters in attendance. The podium was especially constructed for the occasion, built at a height of three-feet-six-inches so as not to overwhelm the diminutive mayor-elect. This time Fred Trump, who did not like backing losers, was on the right side. Following the election, *The New York Times* applauded the Beame victory but warned that if it meant a "resurgence of the old-style machine politics" it would be tragic.

The celebration at the Biltmore had scarcely ended when Fred and Donald Trump applied to the city for a zoning change in an area they wanted to build on just outside Jamaica Estates. They owned a 75,000-

square-foot piece of land on Hillside Avenue between Midland Parkway and Avon Street. Current zoning law restricted the number of apartment units that could be built there; the Trumps wanted it changed so that they could put up a structure with commercial rentals on street level plus an 18-story tower with 290 apartments above. Their intention was to build the complex in conjunction with the New York City Housing and Development Authority at a cost of between $9 million and $13 million. Financing would come from the state, along with the customary package of tax abatements and other inducements. Some local residents opposed the concept on the grounds that it would create "too much density" in an already overcrowded neighborhood. It was an old argument, and still goes on today. No action would be taken on their application for a zoning change by the lame-duck Lindsay administration. It would, however, be one of the first pieces of business facing the new mayor after he took his oath of office in January.

16

Enter Roy M. Cohn, formerly chief counsel to Senator Joseph McCarthy and investigator in the U.S. Attorney's office during the trial of Julius and Ethel Rosenberg, indicted but acquitted three times on charges of conspiracy, bribery, and fraud.

The year 1973 was also Roy Cohn's twenty-fifth anniversary as an attorney. To celebrate the occasion, several hundred of his closest friends decided to honor him with a black-tie dinner in the Grand Ballroom of the Biltmore Hotel. The affair was held on Thursday evening, November 29, a few weeks after Abe Beame's election as mayor. President Richard M. Nixon sent a letter to the hotel, congratulating Cohn for his twenty-five years of public service. Tickets to the dinner were somewhat pricey but tax deductible, since proceeds from the affair were earmarked for two charitable organizations: the Cardinal Spellman Foundation and the American Jewish League Against

Communism. Among the attendees were columnist, author, and ex-mayoral candidate William F. Buckley, Jr.; Monsignor Theodore McCarrick, representing Terrence Cardinal Cooke; Carmine G. DeSapio, former New York County Democratic Party leader; State Supreme Court Justice John M. Murtagh; Mayor-elect Abraham Beame; and Donald Trump, who had met Mr. Cohn at Le Club, one of the posh eastside clubs they both frequented.

William F. Buckley, Jr., ascended to the podium. "Roy Cohn," he said, "is a man who has triumphed over his tormentors, and he deserves the credit we are here to give him so enthusiastically." Other dignitaries took their places at the microphone to extol the attorney. At last Roy Cohn walked to the podium in the midst of solid applause. He thanked those who had turned out to honor him: "It's wonderful to be with my friends," he said. "There is such a wide range of political opinion here. We all tolerate each other in true friendship. All in all, this country has been very kind to me. I'm a grateful man."

Two weeks after the dinner at the Biltmore, following the advice of his friend and attorney Roy Cohn, Donald Trump, acting in his capacity as president of Trump Management Corporation, filed a $100 million lawsuit against the federal government. The Department of Justice, in accusing the Trumps of racial discrimination in their renting policies, had made "irresponsible and baseless charges against the realty company," according to the brief.

Donald apparently believed that the federal government was trying to force the Trumps to rent to welfare cases. "We never discriminated against blacks," Donald had said. "Five to ten percent of our units are rented to blacks in the city. But we won't sign leases with welfare clients unless they have guaranteed income levels, because otherwise, everyone immediately starts leaving the building."

When Donald was questioned about his choice of friends, he said to a *New York Magazine* reporter referring to Cohn, "He's been vicious to others in his protection of me."

Donald Trump was only twenty-seven-years old, but he knew his way around the ring. He knew how to feint, he knew how to jab, he knew when to move in for the knockout. He was well on his way toward achieving his life-long goal of creating an empire based in Manhattan and looking to worlds beyond. For that, however, a queenly partner might well be in order.

Part Three

THE EMPIRE
BUILDER

17

Ivana Zelnickova Winklmayr wasted little time in getting to New York City and making her mark. Immigration laws, however, forced one to take a more roundabout route. Canada was more open to European emigres than the United States; Montreal was the most suitable location for entry into the free world.

The French atmosphere of Quebec, plus the cold Canadian winters, agreed with Ivana. Montreal was more European than American, and the French she spoke in Europe was more than adequate preparation for the patois spoken in Canada. At age twenty-three she was tall, slim, strikingly attractive. When she smiled she looked a bit like a Teutonic version of a young Rita Hayworth. Her most immediately marketable skill was her ability as a skier, and she had no difficulty finding employment as a ski instructor in the Laurentians just north of the city.

One of her close friends in Montreal was a model, and it was at her suggestion that Ivana decided to try that field herself. Others had told her that she was a natural, and the money was considerably better than what she was earning as a weekend ski instructor. The first time she walked into the Audrey Morris agency in Montreal there was little doubt in anyone's mind that she had come to the right place.

"I wish ten more like her would walk in the door right now," Kevin Johnson, the director of the agency, said to me in 1984. "She was just right. She was the perfect height and size and she had a good head for fashion."

Within months Ivana was appearing in fashion shows and her face and figure adorned the pages of Canada's top women's magazines. In her spare time she worked hard to improve her English. It was only a matter of time before she found her way to New York City. Like the man she seemed almost destined to marry, she was attractive, apparently determined, and on her way.

"I'm not only Donald's lawyer but also one of his close friends," said Roy Cohn to Howard Blum of *The New York Times*, as reported in his August 16, 1980 article. "Donald wishes he didn't have to give money to politicians, but he knows it's part of the game. He doesn't try to get anything for it. He's just doing what a lot of people in the real estate business try to do."

Donating money to political campaigns has indeed long been a recognized prerequisite for accomplishing anything in the real estate business. For example, FHA loans from the federal government and low-interest loans under the Mitchell-Lama Law were supposed to be earmarked for developers who were building low- and middle-income housing or perhaps a regional shopping center in such places as Sheepshead Bay, Bensonhurst, or Bay Ridge. Nobody knew that better than Donald Trump. It was just a way of doing business.

THE EMPIRE BUILDER

Donald's plans for a hundred acres of landfill just south of Shore Parkway that the Trump organization owned called for the construction of 10,000 luxury apartments or, in lieu of that, a vast regional shopping center. The land a half mile east of the Verrazano-Narrows Bridge (everyone called it the Verrazano Bridge now), running from Bay 44th Street to 24th Avenue, was created during the construction of the bridge, and the Trumps bought it from the estate of the late Barney Turecamo for $15 million. But, according to a *New York Times* report, Donald did not intend to put up housing without federal funding. Without it the area could not sustain even luxury rents, he believed.

Donald did not invent the rules. But as long as they existed, he knew he had to play by them if he expected to accomplish anything.

"You would be wasting time and paper," said Federal Judge Edward R. Neaher on Friday, January 25, 1974, in dismissing Trump Management's $100 million lawsuit against the government. Instead, he directed Trump Management Corporation to answer government charges that it discriminated against blacks in its renting policies.

The new year was not starting the way Donald Trump would have liked, and the publicity he was getting did not quite square with the image of a rich, successful, swashbuckling empire builder. His father was still trying to tug him back to Brooklyn and Queens. Each time he strained at the bit, urging his father toward the main arena in Manhattan, Fred tried to pull him back toward those other deals on the edge of the city. Over a year had gone by since they had first announced their plan to build a high-rise on Third Avenue. It was still an announcement of intent. It was difficult to convince the world that one had "flair" and "elan" when what the newspapers were talking about was alleged discrimination and patronage.

To put this era of his life behind him, and to get on with the kind of career he truly envisioned for himself, Donald eventually agreed to a compromise with the federal government. He still refused to rent to welfare cases, but he did consent to give the Urban League a weekly

89

list of all vacancies in the family's buildings and to allow that civil rights organization to provide the names of qualified blacks for one out of five of the units in buildings where blacks occupied fewer than 10 percent of the total units. Donald commented that the agreement was to his "full satisfaction" because, among other things, it did not contain "any requirement that would compel Trump Management to accept persons on welfare as tenants unless they were as qualified as any other tenant." He also emphasized that he did not acknowledge any prior discrimination in settling with the government, nor was he obliged to.

It was a way out for both parties. The government showed it was capable of flashing its teeth, if not actually sinking them in, and Donald was able to save face and indeed state later that he had "won" in his confrontation with Uncle Sam. Indeed, to a very great extent he had.

18

Donald would not be denied. Opportunity presented itself in a major way in the corporate personage of the financially destitute Penn Central Transportation Company. Penn Central, the mammoth railroad enterprise and conglomerate, was on the ropes. It had been hemorrhaging money for years past and was now in receivership. The nation itself was in the throes of a demoralizing recession (none dared called it a depression), and New York City was as hard hit as any other area of the country. There was even talk that the city might have to default on its bonds. Unthinkable. Municipal bonds, ostensibly the second most secure investment after obligations of the United States Treasury, suddenly might not be worth the paper they were printed on. Donald smelled blood—translation: opportunity—and he moved in.

On July 29, 1974, he announced that Trump Enterprises, another family corporation, had secured options to buy two of Penn Central's huge waterfront parcels along the Hudson River for $62 million. The first site was located between the river and West End Avenue, and extended from West 59th Street to West 72nd Street. The second ran from West 30th to West 39th streets between the Hudson River and Tenth Avenue at one point and Eleventh Avenue at another. Penn Central could no longer afford to hold onto the properties that encompassed old freight yards, rundown warehouses, and long stretches of abandoned buildings.

The proposed acquisition was mind-boggling even to long-established Manhattan real estate barons. In one action, Donald was planning to buy two enormous tracts of westside Manhattan real estate, a thirteen-block strip in one instance and a nine-block strip in the other, for Depression-era prices. In a booming economy the parcels would be worth several times the agreed-upon purchase price. The point was, of course, that very few people were willing to gamble on a New York City rebound in 1974. Donald Trump was. The barons were lying low. Zeckendorf was still struggling. Helmsley, the Fisher brothers, the Rudins, Sylvan Lawrence, the Tishmans, the Roses, none of them would go near the spot until they had a chance to see which way the economic wind was blowing. What could you do with the westside of Manhattan if the country plummeted into a decade-long depression, with real estate values declining even further? So the kid wanted to gobble up two vast chunks of Manhattan real estate. So what would he do with them? Precisely the kind of conventional wisdom that Donald welcomed, that gave him his opening.

He lost no time in announcing that his plans for the first site, directly west of Lincoln Center, called for the construction of 20,000 luxury and upper-middle-income apartment units renting for $115 to $125 a room, a not inconsiderable amount of money at the time. On the second parcel he would build more of the same, perhaps as many as 10,000 units in a similar rent range. In one stroke the twenty-eight-year-old kid from Queens was proposing to more than double the Trump barony from 24,000 to over 50,000 units. He was laying his claim to empire while still wet behind the ears, at least to the veteran developers' way of thinking.

Of course, turning his vision into reality was going to be considerably more difficult than talking about it. First, the plan had to be approved by the Federal District Court in Philadelphia, which was presiding over Penn Central's chapter-eleven bankruptcy proceedings. Then Donald would need city approval for a zoning change before he could actually start building. Even these high rents, Donald said, could not sustain the projects without some sort of public assistance; soaring construction costs would eat up most of the profits. Donald wanted a long-term loan with low interest rates, preferably under the guidelines of the Mitchell-Lama Law. He would also need substantial tax abatements to make the whole deal worthwhile. But why not? he reasoned. He, unlike his nay-saying elders, was willing to take a chance and bet on Manhattan, take a gamble and help revitalize the city. So why shouldn't the state and city help him out? When Abe Beame was asked for his opinion, he said, according to Donald, "I am happy that Penn Central was willing to give up the property for development."

Mayor Beame, speaking for himself, was more restrained, saying that he would be unable to comment on the deal "until the Board of Estimate had a chance to look it over." Well, fine, if that was the way he wanted it publicly. But in any case there was still the problem of the administration in Albany. Malcolm Wilson, the Republican who had assumed the governor's office when Nelson Rockefeller went to Washington to become vice-president, was not all that friendly to the Trumps or, for that matter, to New York City. One could only hope that in the upcoming election a governor would be put in office with a more appropriate background, like Mayor Beame's—Brooklyn—and a Democrat. A talented and experienced man like Hugh Carey, for example.

19

Speaking of his decision to assign the Penn Central properties to Trump Enterprises, Victor Palmieri, the negotiator responsible for liquidating the company's extensive holdings, said, as reported in *Barron's*:

Those properties were nothing but a black hole of undefinable risk. We interviewed all kinds of people who were interested in them, none of whom had what seemed like the kind of drive and backing and imagination that would be necessary. Until this young guy Trump came along. He's almost a throwback to the 19th century as a promoter. He's larger than life.

Larger than life indeed. Young Donald in his burgundy-colored suits and matching shoes, his initials affixed to his shirts, his cuff links, and license plates so no one would ever overlook who he was, dining at "21" with his date even if "their heads are all screwed on wrong," was definitely working on a larger-than-life image. He was a showman, an artist of sorts whose medium happened to be real estate. Now the barons were paying attention to him, even if they were also waiting for him to fall on his face and go scuttling back to Queens, his tail between his legs. The kid was all talk, brash, arrogant, even obnoxious at times, some of them said. What was he going to *do* with all those rusty freight yards? Luxury apartments in the midst of a depression? He certainly had a mouth on him, all right. But did he know how to build?

"What makes Donald Trump so significant right now," said one Manhattan expert to Judy Klemesrud in *The New York Times*, "is that there is nobody else who is a private promoter on a major scale trying to convince entrepreneurs to develop major pieces of property. If it goes through you could call him the William Zeckendorf of Bad Times."

Donald must have known he was on the right track when he heard the comparison of himself to Zeckendorf, his idol. The living legend was beginning to take shape after all the years of bad press.

"New York is either going to get much better or much worse," said Donald, warming to his theme, "and I think it will get much better."

The older barons were not so easily convinced, however. "In my opinion the jury is still out," said Sam Lefrak in a November 1, 1976, interview with Ms. Klemesrud.

"I just hope he can put his deals together,"said Harry Helmsley.

"His deals are dramatic," commented a Manhattan mortgage banker. "So far the chief beneficiary of his creativity has been his public image."

One investment banker was downright hostile: Trump is "overrated" and "totally obnoxious," he sniffed in the same *New York Times* account.

The new William Zeckendorf, or just an overrated and obnoxious brat? Donald had put himself in the position of the lone stranger who sits down at the table with the shrewdest poker players in town. Lone Hand Donald. High noon. Everybody was watching him deal, but nobody had seen him win a pot. Overnight Donald had made one of the largest single real estate acquisitions on record. He now controlled two major chunks of the westside of Manhattan.

Fine. But if a developer were going to accomplish something with the Penn Central properties, logically he was going to need more political leverage. Having a reasonable mayor in City Hall was great if one were building houses in Queens, but a responsive governor in Albany was even more critical for someone who wanted to make it truly big in Manhattan. The gubernatorial race in 1974 was shaping up to be a close contest between Brooklyn Democrat Hugh Carey and upstate Republican Malcolm Wilson, a sobersided banker-type with jug-handle ears. For good measure there was a smattering of third-party candidates, including one from the Free Libertarian Party named Jerome Tuccille, who ran on a platform to stamp out what he termed idiocracy, or government by idiots. Tuccille called for an end to expanding government and for lower taxes. In a misguided effort to gain publicity for his campaign the Free Libertarian candidate paraded a girl in flesh-colored body stocking on horseback along Central Park South, and gave away free frankfurters with a small bite taken out in front of City Hall in protest against the city's so-called hotdog tax. Tuccille did not accept campaign donations from Donald Trump. Then again, at that time he did not know the Trumps existed, and they had an equal nonawareness of him.

Closing the gap on Malcolm Wilson in the polls was the candidate of the Democratic Party and a graduate of the Madison Club in Brooklyn, Representative Hugh Leo Carey. Carey was born in Brooklyn on April 11, 1919, the son of an oil distributor named Dennis Carey. After a stint with the 104th Infantry during World War II, Major Hugh Carey returned to Brooklyn and graduated from St. John's Law School. Shortly thereafter he married Helen Owen, a widow with a daughter from her first marriage. Hugh and Helen produced thirteen children of their own and kept moving, of necessity, to larger and larger apartments in Brooklyn, eventually ending in the Park Slope section of that borough.

Carey was first elected to office in 1960 as a congressman from a predominantly Republican district in Brooklyn that no other Democrat considered worth running in. The candidacy was his for the asking since the Democrats had grown tired of watching some of their best candidates automatically go down to defeat against incumbent Republicans. Carey's upset victory came in the wake of John F. Kennedy's photo finish ahead of Richard Nixon in the presidential race the same year. Once in office reelection turned out to be relatively easy for Carey during the Democratic decade of the sixties. Tragedy, however, struck the Carey family with the loss of two of their sons, Peter and Hugh, in an automobile accident. And it visited the congressman again when his wife Helen was struck down by cancer in March 1974, shortly after he announced his candidacy for governor.

Hugh Leo Carey was a rotund, red-faced man with mostly gray hair at the beginning of the campaign. By midsummer he was considerably slimmer, and his mostly gray hair had taken on a somewhat darker hue. By election eve, though not exactly svelte, he had managed to shed thirty pounds, noticeably from his midsection, and there was scarcely a gray hair to be seen among the black.

It is, of course, hardly accurate to suggest that Carey's physical transformation was responsible for his humiliation of Rockefeller stand-in Malcolm Wilson. Carey had a good record and he campaigned well. Wilson was a lackluster politician. In any case, the voters of New York elected Carey in a landslide on November 5, 1974, less than a week after another knockout—Muhammad Ali's of George Foreman in the eighth round to recapture the heavyweight championship. The final tally was 2,888,246 votes for Carey and 2,103,187 for Wilson, 58 percent of the vote to Wilson's 42 percent. (Tuccille, by the way, came in an *extremely* distant third with scarcely over 11,000 votes.) At the victory celebration at the Commodore Hotel, Carey said to an uproarious crowd:

"We've won the campaign to get our government back in the hands of the people of New York."

In the course of doing so, Governor-elect Carey had accumulated a campaign debt of $2.3 million, including a $1.2 million loan from his brother Edward, an oilman like their father; the other loans came mostly from an assortment of unions, real estate developers, and contractors. Wilson's contributors included the financial institutions around the state, primarily the banks, insurance companies, and, curiously, the racetracks. So the divisions in the campaign seemed clearly drawn— the unions and real estate interests in one camp, the pin-striped suits and racetrack moguls in the other. On Election Day, in Carey's words, "the people" somehow had won.

Hugh Carey's election ended sixteen years of Republican Party rule in New York State, and gave the Democrats control of the State Assembly in addition to the State House. It also positioned the Madison Club as the most powerful Democratic organization in the state as well as in New York City. A year earlier, when Abe Beame was being sworn in as mayor, Stanley Steingut's mother remarked to him, "Your father in heaven must be smiling today to see Abe Beame being sworn in by Pat Sobel." Stanley Steingut was the Speaker of the State Assembly, and his father, Irwin, had run the Madison Club until his death. Abe Beame was Irwin Steingut's accountant and Sobel was his lawyer. Now, on November 5, 1974, Stanley Steingut was able to smile back at his mother and say about Carey, "Hugh is one of us."

Immediately after the election Governor-elect Hugh Carey appointed a six-member executive finance committee to help him reduce his campaign debt. The director of the committee was Louise Sunshine, Carey's chief fund-raiser during the campaign, a hard-driving ball of energy and president of a real estate company called the Nelson Development Corporation. A few weeks later Carey formed a task force to study housing problems in the state. Among its appointees were those two friendly adversaries from Queens, Samuel Lefrak and Donald John Trump.

20

Donald was now a major league player. His acquisition of the Penn Central properties, together with his appointment to Governor Carey's housing commission, served notice that he was well positioned to compete with the superbarons. His youth, his flamboyant style and way of life made him a curiosity in a world dominated by elderly men in gray suits who preferred to maintain a low profile with the public. *Still* only twenty-eight years old, Donald had already come a long way from Brooklyn and Queens and, it seemed, was well on his way toward launching the career he'd long dreamed of.

But the past, as they say, has a way of coming back to haunt us, often at the most inopportune moments. Hardly had Donald's quiet appointment to the new governor's task force taken place when a new incident occurred involving the old Steeplechase Park site in Coney Island. A group of city officials declared that the city had made a mistake in 1969 when it agreed to pay Fred Trump $4 million for the property. Abraham Beame had become comptroller at the time. Making a bad deal even worse, they claimed, Steeplechase had been leased to a park owner named Norman Kaufman for $20,000 a year since the acquisition—a pittance compared to the $158,000 a year the city should have been getting for the land. It was no accident, said Stern, that Kaufman was a buddy of Abraham Lindenbaum who, in turn, was one of Abe Beame's closest friends. The councilman urged the city to abandon its "ludicrous" plan to build a park and refurbish the area for a public housing project. Mayor Beame promised to appoint a task force to study the problem. Fred Trump was not available for comment. Donald was: "There's such a preponderance of low-income housing [in the neighborhood already that] people just don't want to *go* there anymore," said he.

Meanwhile, Donald's rapid emergence as the rising star of the Trump barony was conceivably having its effect on his brothers. Maryanne was diligently working her way up the judicial ladder, and was said by many to be one of the most influential women in her field, just a notch behind Sandra Day O'Connor. Fred Trump, Jr., however, was not faring well at all. Insecure and troubled to begin with, his marriage was beginning to fall apart and he moved to Florida, where he got a job working on charter boats.

Elizabeth continued to work as a secretary at the Chase Manhattan Bank. She observed her kid brother with an older sister's eye, marveling to me about his bravado and intelligence. The "brat" just might grow up to be somebody after all. Robert, the youngest, was following, if a bit haltingly, in Donald's footsteps. Lacking his brother's flair and imagination, he nevertheless was working as a vice-president under Donald in the Trump organization. He even moved to the eastside of Manhattan and took an apartment in the same building where Donald lived.

* * *

Ivana Winklmayr arrived in Canada jobless and homeless but also tall, blonde, and gorgeous.

In Montreal Ivana was able to become one of Canada's top models in a short time. Doors were being opened.

Who knew? Perhaps she would meet someone really special. Someone for example, like Donald Trump.

21

In March 1975 U.S. District Court Judge John P. Fullam made it official when he approved the sale of the Penn Central sites to Trump Enterprises for $62 million. According to the terms of the deal, Penn Central would retain up to a 25 percent interest in any projects Trump erected on the gargantuan westside parcels. Donald Trump, president of Trump Enterprises, lost no time in pronouncing the sale "a marvelous deal" for the bankrupt conglomerate. "Penn Central could reap as much as $300 million from this," he said.

Donald said that the construction of the two enormous housing projects would take as long as ten years and cost over a billion dollars, but it would provide "tens of thousands of jobs" for idle construction workers, and he hoped to begin building within eighteen to twenty-four months, just as soon as he obtained the zoning changes he needed and secured an agreeable financial package from the City Planning Commission. "As of now I'd probably lean toward Mitchell-Lama," Donald said. Not a surprise.

The true brilliance of this deal soon emerged, and when it did the New York superbarons quickly realized that Donald Trump, not yet twenty-nine years of age, was perhaps one of the best negotiators of his or any age. On the surface he was acquiring two huge tracts of Manhattan real estate for $62 million, a cheap enough price in itself. In reality, Penn Central would not receive any cash immediately for the sites; the $62 million was to be paid out over the next few years as the land was cleared and developed. Later, if Penn Central exercised its option to buy into the properties, it would receive 25 percent of the profits from the buildings, but by Donald's own calculations this was at least a decade in the future. In effect, Donald John Trump had secured the right to buy two large hunks of Manhattan real estate for $62 million without laying a nickel out-of-pocket. The properties were his for a handshake and a promise of future profits—none of which would be forthcoming if he failed to get the kind of financing and zoning changes he wanted from the city and state.

Awesome. Was the kid, asked the shaking older heads, some kind of a genius, or did he somehow have everybody who counted supporting him? What did Victor Palmieri, the negotiator for Penn Central, have to say about it? "Whether Donald is charming his way or bulling his way through a deal, he makes things happen in an almost impossible environment."

For his part Donald refused to take any credit for having pulled off perhaps the financial coup of the decade.

"What happened I guess is that this was a time when nobody was even thinking of building, and here I am proposing to build something."

Simple. But a stunner to the superbarons. Here was Penn Central Transportation Company in bankruptcy, starved for cash, and it comes away from the bargaining table minus two of its most valuable pieces of property—and no cash. With nothing to show for the deal except a promise. Even Samuel Lefrak was forced to reassess Fred Trump's son and to admit that "he's bold, very daring and swashbuckling."

Whatever he was, Donald J. Trump was certainly being noticed and talked about by everybody who mattered. Representative Bella Abzug, another larger-than-life personality, was not quite sure what to make of the situation, but she was an astute enough politician to know that some sort of an opinion was called for. With one of her wide-brimmed hats flapping in the wind, she proclaimed that she was neither for nor against the proposal until she had a chance to study its impact on traffic problems in the area and its effect on air pollution. "If he intends to put up luxury housing all the way through, then I'm opposed to it," she added with emphasis, putting herself on the side of "the people" on the issue. It was a safe enough position, one sure to offend as few people as possible.

While the dust was still flying and everyone was punching his calculator in an attempt to figure out the winners and losers in the deal, and especially what it all meant as far as the city was concerned, Donald Trump dropped yet another bombshell on the real estate world. In May he announced that Trump Enterprises, together with the Hyatt hotel chain, had arranged to buy from Penn Central the Commodore Hotel adjoining Grand Central Terminal. The Commodore was a fifty-nine-year-old run-down structure that had been losing $1.5 million a year for its owner. It was the least successful of all the hotels the conglomerate Penn Central owned in New York, which included the Barclay, the Biltmore, and the Roosevelt.

At first glance the terms of this deal did not seem as lucrative for Trump as his westside land deal. Penn Central was actually going to get paid some money for the moribund Commodore, $10 million as it turned out. Donald's own father, in fact, had been against the purchase from the start: "I told Donald that buying the Commodore at a time when even the Chrysler Building was in receivership was like fighting for a seat on the Titanic. But he insisted, and in the end he was right."

Fred, though, was more concerned at the time about getting the

105

Board of Estimate to approve the construction of a McDonald's on some land he owned in Coney Island that was originally supposed to be a parking lot for the tenants at Trump Village. Donald just could not get the old tiger to change his stripes.

As for Donald's latest deal, the more the experts crunched the numbers, the more they realized that Donald had walked away from this negotiating session too in a virtual no-lose position. His keys to success here were, first, taking in a partner with deep pockets who was even hungrier for the hotel than he was and, second, tying in a request for a tax abatement (already worked out eight months earlier with city officials, although no one knew it as yet) that would guarantee him tens of millions of dollars during the rest of his lifetime.

According to the terms Donald worked out with Palmieri, Penn Central would receive $10 million for the Commodore, $6 million of which would go immediately to New York City in payment of delinquent taxes. Donald would then sell the hotel to the Urban Development Corporation for one dollar with the provision that the UDC would lease it back to him and the Hyatt Corporation for ninety-nine years, at which time the property would revert to the city's control. The reason for this was that the condemnation powers of the UDC were required to evict holdout tenants in the Commodore who refused to move voluntarily. Donald and his partner were committed to pay the city $250,000 a year in rent after the new hotel opened for business, with payments eventually escalating to $2,775,000 annually over the years. At the time, Donald estimated it would cost about $70 million to build the new hotel. He did not mention it then, but the cost of refurbishing the facade of Grand Central Terminal next door was to be paid out of a public improvements fund. Hyatt was to receive a management fee amounting to 4 percent of the gross, and a 20 percent share of the profits. Joseph Amoroso, the executive vice-president of Hyatt, who hammered out most of the details with Trump, believed the new Grand Hyatt could be ready by 1978. He was especially pleased because this would be Hyatt's first hotel in New York City. Since Donald immediately mortgaged the building for more than he was paying for it, he had in effect bought himself a hotel in midtown Manhattan for zero dollars out-of-pocket.

The financial structure of the purchase was complicated, and the immediate benefit to Donald was not all that apparent to the Manhattan barons who analyzed it so closely. Granted, Donald and his partner had bought a hotel cheaply. But it had been a money-loser for years past, and there was no guarantee that they would ever be able to pull a profit out of it later on. It was not until news of Donald's special tax-abatement deal with the city started to emerge that it finally made sense to everyone.

Before he even sat down to negotiate with Penn Central, Donald had gotten Mayor Beame's support for the first tax abatement in New York City history for commercial property. Under Beame's leadership, the city passed something called the Business Investment Incentive Policy, and Donald was to be its first beneficiary. The linchpin of the Commodore Hotel deal, as the public was beginning to learn, was a proposed 100 percent abatement on all property taxes for forty years. Since taxes on the Commodore in 1975 came to about $4 million a year, the minimum value of Donald's tax break amounted to $160 million. (The estimated taxes on the Grand Hyatt ten years later were $9 million a year, pushing Donald's windfall into the $300 to 400 million class over forty years.) Of a sudden, the Manhattan developers understood all too well how Donald Trump could guarantee the city a minimum of $250,000 a year in rental income and make a profit for himself and his partner. It was easy, even at Depression-era hotel rates, when one was already saving $4 million a year before you opened the doors to the public.

The outcry from other Manhattan developers who felt they were being put at a disadvantage, and from city officials who had opposed Beame's investment incentive policy, reverberated beyond the city.

"Clearly, the city could be getting a better deal," commented Deputy Mayor Robert F. Wagner, Jr., son of the former mayor, according to *The New York Times*. "But Donald Trump did make his deal at a time when the city was desperate for development. Nobody was building hotels in Manhattan."

Another Manhattan developer, who was struggling along without any special tax advantages, claimed in an interview with Judy Klemesrud that Donald was "on the threshold of the greatest real estate coup of the last miserable three years."

Der Scutt, the architect who had worked with Donald on other projects and helped him decorate his penthouse apartment, was more approving. "That Donald," he said to me, "he could sell sand to the Arabs and refrigerators to the Eskimos."

City Councilman Henry J. Stern said: "Donald Trump runs with the same clique that continues to manipulate things behind the scenes in this city," he said to Howard Blum. "He has ties through his father to the Brooklyn Democratic machine that produced Hugh Carey. Roy Cohn is his lawyer. He throws around a lot of money in political campaigns." (Stern was speaking in the context of the proposed New York City convention center.)

Donald Trump viewed the situation otherwise. "The city's a disaster," he said. "Everyone believes it's going to get worse. But I'm the only one who believes the opposite. I'm the only one who's willing to buy the Commodore."

"Yes. But why is the city willing to give you a forty-year tax abatement?" he was asked by Howard Tell of *Barron's*.

Donald reflected a moment, a smile, one suspects, developing along the corner of his mouth.

"Because I didn't ask for fifty," he answered.

22

Actually, the way things were going Donald Trump might never have to build a thing. He was bringing in piles of money on the strength of his deals alone. He had rapidly elevated himself to the world of the super-rich in the brief seven years since he graduated from the Wharton Business School. They were talking about him now, his name was suddenly being celebrated across the entire country. For the first time, the Manhattan real estate barons regarded him as a formidable competitor. But money alone would never be enough to satisfy Donald Trump. *He* knew he could create unique buildings, structures that everyone else would stand back and admire. He would not be happy until others were convinced of this as well.

As for his social life, it was better than ever. He was invited where it counted. His association with Roy Cohn was obviously a social asset. Now he was invited to dinner parties and other social events on the strength of his own reputation. He no longer required others to open doors for him.

It was at a party in Montreal during a skiing vacation that, in true storybook fashion, they met. One can easily visualize the following scenario: He noticed a tall, beautiful blonde across a crowded room. But it was more than her beauty that made him take particular notice of her. She had a European accent for one thing, although he could not place it exactly. When he moved over to talk to her, he quickly decided that she was quietly intelligent, never mind her halting English. A depth and seriousness transcended the language barrier. She appeared to have more substance than most of the young women he encountered, a deeper purpose in life than merely flaunting her beauty. She was also somewhat shy, a trait not customarily associated with the pretty young climbers he met at such parties. They hit it off immediately. For the first time in a long while, Donald Trump had met a beautiful woman who had her head screwed on right.

During the next few months they saw each other at every opportunity. Ivana had to travel to Manhattan. Donald urged her to make the trip as frequently as possible, and she was more than willing. He enjoyed being with her, talking to her about his goals and ambitions, and Ivana mixed well with the friends he introduced her to in New York. He especially liked it that she came from a middle-class background, was sensible and down-to-earth. Her father was an electrical engineer; she grew up reading blueprints over his shoulder in the evenings. She was accustomed to hard work and perseverance, all the virtues Fred Trump had tried to instill in his own children. Donald was also not unaware that his wealth made him something of a catch for many young women, and he found Ivana understanding when he told her about his friends who had been "taken to the cleaners" by designing women. She understood his predicament, and did not press him to marry her. If anything, Donald was more pursuer than pursued, or at least so it appeared as he spent ever greater amounts of time with Ivana.

Fred Trump noticed the change in his son from the start, and was both amused by and approving of his infatuation with the model from Montreal. He liked Ivana and agreed with Donald's assessment of her good sense and practicality:

"Donald folded up like an umbrella the first time he saw her." Fred laughed about it later on.

"We knew it was serious," Roy Cohn agreed, "when Donald started picking her up at the airport himself."

Not only had Ivana met someone rich and successful, she had turned the head of one of the most celebrated young businessmen of the time, a man who was the focal point of controversial hundred-million-dollar deals. Incredibly enough, he was tall, lean, and movie-star handsome in the bargain, and his face and name were currently being spread all over the newspapers and magazines. Not only did such a man invite her to visit his city, the city of her girlhood fantasies, as often as she could, but he met her at the airport in a chauffeur-driven limousine. For Ivana, it was a fairy tale come true.

Ivana Zelnickova Winklmayr was not, however, the only woman who played a serious role in Donald Trump's life at this time. During Hugh Carey's successful gubernatorial campaign the previous year, Donald became impressed with the talents of Louise Sunshine, Carey's chief fund raiser. Hugh Carey depended on her more than on any of his aides. She controlled the money and therefore the power, or the source of the power, within the new governor's organization. Since the election she had retained her critical position as Carey's top assistant. Louise Sunshine was the one who orchestrated a series of events to help the governor pay off his campaign debt—an evening of entertainment at Lincoln Center, a Victory Ball at the Waldorf-Astoria, a dinner dance at Pier 90; there was no end to her ingenuity and industry. Louise had also been appointed to the more prestigious post of treasurer of the New York State Democratic Party.

Donald apparently decided that the next best thing to having a hotline to the governor's mansion was having Louise Sunshine in his employ. So he offered her a job with the Trump organization at something like five times the salary she would be making in the public arena. She retained her position with the state Democratic Party at the same time.

Donald had already abandoned his idea of building luxury apartments on the second parcel of land he had acquired from Penn Central, the one running from West 30th to West 39th streets along the Hudson River. He now had better plans for that land that would be far more lucrative and far less risky than putting up luxury housing in the prevailing economic climate of the city. To help him accomplish it he turned to Louise Sunshine.

"Donald is always beaming and scheming," Ivana told me that she had joked to his younger brother, Robert, one evening.

"Wheeling and dealing," he corrected her good-naturedly. "Wheeling and dealing is the expression."

"Wheeling and dealing, beaming and scheming. Is all the same, no?"

Sports executives attending New York *Post* forum held in December 1983. From left: Donald Trump, New Jersey Generals; Fred Wilpon, New York Mets; Sonny Werblin, Madison Square Garden; and George Steinbrenner, New York Yankees.

Former Governor of New York Hugh Carey, Mrs. Carey, Ivana and Donald Trump at Trump Tower in December 1984.

ABOVE: Donald and his father, Fred Trump, with Mayor Edward Koch in July 1982.

BELOW: Donald and Ivana stepping out in September 1984.

Christmas shoppers crowd Trump Tower in November 1984.

RIGHT: Donald Trump is the main speaker at the March, 1984 press conference for the new Harrah's casino at Trump Plaza in Atlantic City.

BELOW: Donald Trump shakes hands with Herschel Walker at March, 1984 press conference after announcing Walker's signing a $6 million, four-year contract to play for the New Jersey Generals.

ABOVE: The Trumps at home in their apartment overlooking Central Park before they moved into Trump Tower.

BELOW: Donald Trump in his office during a 1984 interview...

...and atop his "T" in the atrium of Trump Tower.

Trump Plaza on Third Avenue as it looked in 1984.

Donald Trump and his father, Fred, as they contemplated entering the Manhattan real estate market in 1973.

The Trumps' weekend retreat in Greenwich, Connecticut, 1982.

OPPOSITE PAGE: Donald Trump's Grand Hyatt, the site of the old Commodore Hotel, on Forty-second Street in New York City.

ABOVE: Donald Trump announces plans for New York City convention center, 1976.

BELOW: Donald getting into his "initialized" limousine in front of his apartment building at 160 East 65th Street in 1976.

23

In December 1975, a few months after his twenty-ninth birthday, Donald announced for the first time his new plans for the nine-block spread west of Tenth Avenue. Instead of luxury housing for the area, he would build a massive convention center. "It would be the largest convention center in the world," he said, although this turned out to be another example of his salesmanship and hyperbole. Der Scutt, whom Donald chose to design the center, told me: "Donald is extremely aggressive when he sells, maybe to the point of overselling. Like he'll say the convention center is going to be the biggest in the world when it really isn't. He'll exaggerate for the purpose of making a sale."

Not, of course, exactly a capital crime. Both the state and city had been contemplating the construction of a major convention center in New York for several years past, and at this point had more or less decided to locate it at one of two locations: a large tract of land in the

West 40s owned by Preston Robert Tisch, or another vacant spread of land in Battery Park at the foot of Manhattan. Donald's bid to have his own parcel in the West 30s picked as the site put him in direct conflict with Tisch, whose feathers he had ruffled a few months earlier with his proposed tax abatement for the Commodore. Donald claimed that he could erect the convention hall in fourteen months for $110 million, more quickly and less expensively than Tisch's estimate for his own project. Donald had also lined up some critical support before going public with his proposal.

"Putting the New York Convention Center in Battery Park is like putting a nightclub in a graveyard," said Theodore Kheel, the powerful labor negotiator, in defense of Donald's bid. According to Kheel, the West 30s would be the best location because the center would be close to shops, hotels, and restaurants, and it would serve as "a catalyst for a resurgence of business activity in midtown." Mayor Beame, when asked for his opinion on the matter, stated that he had been in favor of the Battery Park location but would have to review the situation. Preston Robert Tisch listened to all this in dismay. He sensed that the battle was slipping away from him. With Governor Carey yet to be heard from, the handwriting on the wall was starting to appear more clearly. It was not an easy outcome for Tisch to accept since he had been strongly in the running before the 1973 and 1974 elections. Despite this unsettling turn of events, he managed to maintain his composure when asked to evaluate Donald Trump's skills as a negotiator: "He's a very bright and capable real estate man," Tisch said diplomatically. He knew how to handle defeat like a pro.

"I feel a new convention center in Manhattan will be a turning point for the city," said Donald Trump, looking to close the sale. "It will get rid of all that pornographic garbage in Times Square. Psychologically, I think it will resurge and rejuvenate the city."

Donald maintained that he had decided against going ahead with his original plan for luxury housing in the area because of the dreary economic conditions pervading the country. "If the Democrats get elected in 1976," he said, "there will be $20 billion in housing programs. If the Republicans get in there will be a drought for years." Developing his theme further, he said that federal subsidies were required to build apartments profitably on the Penn Central location, and none was currently forthcoming from the administration in Washington. President Ford, it should be recalled, was setting something of a record vetoing one spending bill after another.

"But I'm a young guy," Donald said. "Eventually there will be a big housing program. Meanwhile I also plan to build the world's largest hotel-casino in Las Vegas. It will be called Xanadu."

The casino he did finally build was in Atlantic City, not Las Vegas, and it would be known by a different name than Xanadu. But never mind, Donald Trump was on a roll. How could anyone keep up with him? Forty-year tax abatements; a mammoth convention center; and now Xanadu. No sooner had he pulled off one brilliant financial coup than he was announcing another. At the very least it was a clever diversionary tactic. Before his adversaries had an opportunity to regroup their forces and launch a counterattack, he was already moving the battle lines to a new theater of operation. He was *surrounding* the enemy with smoke and mirrors, keeping them disoriented. Yesterday it was the Commodore, today the convention center, tomorrow Xanadu, next week . . . probably not even Donald himself knew that yet.

One thing, however, he must have known for sure: he was building up a full head of steam, roaring ahead faster and faster with the throttle open. Nothing could stop him now.

24

The New Year of 1976 began for Donald with his forces grouped and ready to attack on two major fronts: the lower Penn Central parcel in the West 30s and the Commodore Hotel site on East 42nd Street. The opening salvo was fired on January 2, when David L. Yunich, the chairman of the Metropolitan Transit Authority, declared that he was foursquare behind Donald's proposal to build the New York City Convention Center on West 34th Street near the Hudson River. Donald reinforced this message two days later:

"Any further discussion of Battery Park City for a convention center should be stopped and the facility built in midtown, at 34th Street, where it has almost unanimous support."

Less than three weeks later Donald appeared at a press conference with two key supporters who backed his proposal: Seymour Durst, chairman of the Broadway Association representing more than a hundred banks, businesses, and restaurants in the west midtown area; and Gerald Schoenfeld, the head of the Shubert Organization and a director of the League of New York Theaters and Producers. Together they confronted officials of the Port Authority of New York and New Jersey, who were still advocating the Battery Park location, and accused the city of abandoning midtown Manhattan: "Putting the convention center in the West 30s would give the area a big boost," they announced in a joint communiqué.

Since constructing the center in the West 40s would be so expensive, according to Donald, this left his land as the only logical site on which to build. "I can do it in fourteen months for $125 million," he estimated. No one seemed to notice, but he had suddenly upped the ante by $15 million from the previous month.

While his opponents were gathering their forces and preparing a counteroffensive, Donald immediately deployed his troops to East 42nd Street and launched a second attack—his main one, as it turned out. In the end, as everyone eventually learned, the Commodore was really his overriding passion of the moment. The potential spoils of war in this campaign dwarfed everything else by far.

In February the Penn Central Transportation Company announced that it might have to shut down the Commodore in a few months because of mounting operation costs. Union contracts would have to be renegotiated at that time, and Penn Central was in no position to agree to any wage hikes. It therefore had no alternative but to close the hotel. The threat of a boarded-up Commodore on one of New York's premier pieces of real estate sent shock waves rippling throughout the community.

"We dread the Commodore going dark," declared Nettie Deutsch, vice-president of the Lexington Hotel just a few blocks north of 42nd Street. She said that a darkened Commodore would have a blighting effect that would destroy other businesses in the area.

Alfred Eisenpreis, the city's Economic Development Administrator, concurred with her. "A closed Commodore would have a very serious blighting influence on the east midtown area," he said.

Notch by notch, the screw was turned and the pressure began to mount. Donald Trump's sense of timing and his skilled use of allies were near-impeccable. He was a master tactician, a young Alexander of the real estate world not yet out of his twenties who seized upon an opportunity and knew instinctively, it seemed, how to take advantage of it. As the heat of battle began to build, the Board of Estimate held a meeting to discuss the question of a special tax abatement for the new hotel. Under consideration was a waiver of all taxes on the property. In return the city wanted, as mentioned, $250,000 a year in rent, a figure that would eventually go as high as $4.2 million annually over the years. Paul O'Dwyer, president of the City Council and the brother of the late William O'Dwyer, the mayor of New York in the pre-Wagner days, hailed the concept as "a very exciting hope for the city." It would create 1,500 jobs and would provide the city of New York with a share of the profits, he said. The city, under the terms of the agreement, would receive 10 percent of the first $500,000 of net profits, 12.5 percent of the next million, and 15 percent of everything above $1.5 million. Net profits were to be calculated as profits after debt service and other expenses, a not inconsiderable factor since Donald had already lined up a $72 million construction loan to build his hotel.

The tax abatement, as proposed, was to continue for a period of fifty years. Remember, when Donald was questioned about the city's willingness to grant him a forty-year tax abatement, he whimsically replied that it was only because he hadn't asked for fifty years. As it turned out, his original request had been for fifty years after all. "A project like this would be impossible for any developer without this abatement," Donald elaborated. He defended his position with the claim that New York would reap a minimum of $4 million a year in profits alone, as much as he would have to pay in taxes if the abatement were not granted. It was a good deal for the city, he argued, one that would bring more money into the public till in the long run. The Commodore at the time was charging only $20.50 a day for rooms, and was still operating at a paltry 33 percent occupancy rate. The new Grand Hyatt would command $65 a day on average, said Donald, thus producing more money for the city's coffers. (His prediction, which seemed grandiose at the time, actually turned out to be on the low side. Not even Donald fully anticipated the full extent of New York City's economic recovery that sent hotel prices soaring into the stratosphere by the early 1980s.)

Victor Palmieri rallied to Donald's cause, with his ominous announcement that Penn Central would have no alternative but to shut down the Commodore by the summer at the latest. Five hundred hotel employees would be let go and, by implication, forced onto the already swollen unemployment rolls. Donald Trump, on the other hand, was proposing to put three times that number back to work as soon as his package was approved.

Following this meeting, the gnashing of teeth grew even more ferocious. The battle lines were clearly drawn and the cries of indignation rose. Harry Helmsley, a man who normally kept a low profile and who was certainly no stranger to the hotel business himself, was moved to object: "There probably has to be some sort of incentive, but maybe too much is being given."

Alphonse Salamone, the managing director of the New York Hilton Hotel, was more direct. "Give them a ten-year tax incentive and then let's compete," he said.

Albert Formicola, executive vice-president of the Hotel Association of New York, was opposed to the long-term tax abatement on the grounds that these "incentives are not available to all of us." It would put the other hotels at a disadvantage in competing with the Grand Hyatt, since they already paid the city a total of $50 million a year in property taxes. "There should also be incentives to stay in business for those of us who have been loyal to New York and kept viable," he concluded.

Another developer lamented that "the incentive program would have improved our reception from lenders had it been available earlier."

Mario de Genova, president of the Americana Hotel, was equally upset. "Unless existing hotels receive similar relief," he claimed, "the tax abatement would be immoral and unfair."

The immoral presumably became moral if one shared in it.

Putting it all together, the hoteliers' objections were not so much against the idea of the abatement as against Donald Trump being singled out as the lone beneficiary of it. Donald, of course, had thought of it first and had the pull to make it happen. Not unreasonable criteria for an advantage, he and others might argue.

There was also a cry raised by an assortment of civic groups worried about any one builder being singled out for a "windfall profit." "It is impossible to forecast land and property values and tax rates for as much as fifty years into the future," said one of their spokesmen, speculating that the total value of Donald's proposed abatement could well be far in excess of even the current estimates.

Donald responded to this outpouring with a combination of sales-manship and one-upmanship. On the one hand he alluded to the benefits everyone would enjoy if he got his chance to build his hotel. On the other he intimated that all this might not come to pass if he did not get the terms he wanted. Midtown blight was a fact of life; he was willing to take a chance on the city despite its sorry economic climate. But he would only take that chance on his own terms.

25

Donald Trump now had reached the status of attracting the ire of Ralph Nader in Washington, D.C. Nader, the grim-visaged champion of oppressed consumers across the land, dispatched one of his chief lieutenants to the Big Apple to join forces with Councilmen Henry J. Stern and Robert F. Wagner, Jr. in opposing the tax-incentive plan. The unlikely coalition of Manhattan hotel owners, city politicians, and now a Ralph Nader study group provided the onlooker with more than a dash of irony and bemusement. If politics makes for strange bedfellows, this collection of hoteliers, some of whom looked as though they had stepped from the pages of *The Godfather*, and consumer advocates edged on the bizarre.

Together, they held a press conference on the sidewalk in front of the Commodore, which itself was beginning to take on the aspects of a haunted mansion, to declare that Trump's abatement would result in "excessive tax savings." "The city's history in making complex real estate deals is a sorry one," said Stern.

Mayor Beame's office issued a statement of its own saying that the mayor himself would negotiate with Donald Trump to reduce the proposed tax abatement from fifty to thirty-five years. Beame had many virtues, but few had ever included the art of negotiation among them. Donald's critics were less than impressed.

"Basically, I would be much less interested in the deal if the present tax abatement is reduced," Donald stated, adding for emphasis, "I would not put ten cents into it." This thrust was followed by one from Victor Palmieri, who said, "Mr. Trump is the only developer in the past three years who is interested in the Commodore." He then broke the news that Penn Central was planning to shut down the Commodore for good on Tuesday, May 11, because of mounting operating losses. Palmieri denied that this announcement was designed to raise the specter of economic blight spreading throughout the midtown area like a renascent Black Death. Others were not so sure.

"It seems to me like someone is trying to force the issue," commented William Stuhlberg, the chairman of a local community board.

In any event, the forces were joined, and the battle was finally resolved on Thursday, May 20, when the Board of Estimate gave its unanimous approval for a forty-year tax abatement.

Present at this meeting was a group of commercial tenants in the Commodore who complained that they faced imminent eviction. The members of the Board of Estimate sympathized with their plight and told them to renegotiate their leases with Mr. Trump and the UDC, which was about to become the official owner of the hotel. In return for the forty-year abatement Donald agreed, as mentioned, to pay the city a rent of $250,000 a year, eventually going up to a maximum of $2,775,000 annually after the abatement period was over. New York City would also share the net profits according to the schedule that was made public earlier.

Among all those who had fought Donald on the issue and lost, perhaps none was more bitter than Councilman Stern. "Donald Trump is a transplanted 19th-century swashbuckling entrepreneur," he said, "and it is up to public officials to rein him in. I don't so much fault him for asking the city for things as I do public officials who gave him his way."

For Donald Trump, the final decision of the Board of Estimate was his finest hour to date. He had already proved that he could put together a complex financial deal. Now he would be given the opportunity to show that he could build something as well.

Beaming and scheming, wheeling and dealing. Whatever, Donald was on the verge of making his mark on Manhattan. He'd established a precedent in New York City for developers and in so doing had positioned himself as its major beneficiary. The other builders, at first put out by Donald's apparently special treatment from the city fathers, quickly realized that the new Business Investment Incentive Policy could only help them all in the long run. The kid was doing their work for them.

With his masterful and much-heralded victory in the Commodore campaign now behind him, Donald once again turned his attention back to the furor over the convention site. In June, less than a month following the approval of his financial package by the Board of Estimate, and less than a month before the Democratic National Convention was due to get underway at Madison Square Garden, Donald refuted the Port Authority's contention that the Battery Park location still merited consideration. Battery Park might be suitable, said Donald, if the West Side Highway were already in place and thereby providing people with quick access to the area from midtown Manhattan. But the highway project was hopelessly bogged down. By the most optimistic estimate it would take at least ten years to complete at a cost of over a billion dollars. Meanwhile he was offering his own spread of land in the West 30s where he could build the new convention center for . . . $170 million. Millions versus billions, now versus maybe never.

Still, once again Donald was upping the ante. The previous December he mentioned $110 million as the cost of building the center. A month later his estimate had risen to $125 million. Now, with more and more of the competition out of the way, the estimated construction cost made a leap to $170 million. To be fair, everyone else's cost estimates were skyrocketing as well. So many groups had a vested interest in the proposal that the entire project was turning into an enormous white elephant. At this stage Donald had Theodore Kheel, the westside businessmen's associations, and Mayor Beame in his camp. Governor Carey would soon give his own stamp of approval to the Trump plan. But the chorus of opposition was also getting louder. The closer anyone got to consummating a deal, the more elusive it became. It seemed as though it would go on forever.

Exasperated, Donald redirected his attention to the other Penn Central site further north. With everyone focused on the convention center controversy, he held a press conference to announce his intention to build three clusters of high-rise buildings in the thirteen-block stretch in the West 60s, with rents running $125 to $140 a room. This gambit seemed to take his opposition by surprise. His opponents were planning to zap him over here, but suddenly he was over there. Now you see him, now you don't. Councilman Stern and some members of local community organizations complained about the danger of overloading city facilities, particularly the 72nd Street subway station and sewage capabilities, as well as additional traffic congestion in the neighborhood if Trump were permitted to add so many new apartments there.

Donald was ready for them. "I'm only trying to bring back middle-class residents to the city," he said. "Many of them would probably walk to work in midtown anyway. In any event, the westside subway is not heavily used at present."

Members of a neighborhood organization said that they were in a better position than Donald to judge conditions in the subway system. They moved to block his plans for the high-rise apartment complex in the area, and this proposal too became bogged down in emotional squabbling. In these other Penn Central locations Donald was finding it difficult if not impossible to duplicate his success in the battle over the Commodore.

As the Democratic Convention got underway at Madison Square Garden in the summer of 1976, Donald made his sympathies in the upcoming campaign well-known, complaining publicly about the new law that restricted the amount an individual could contribute to any one candidate.

"I think it's a terrible thing. You should be able to give as much as you want and can afford," he said openly and without apology.

Fred Wertheimer, vice-president of Common Cause, which had been instrumental in getting the new law passed, had a different view: "The old system is gone," he said, "and we're all better off for its demise."

Later events were to show that he was a bit premature in his pronouncement.

26

When Donald Trump turned thirty in August of 1976 he found himself the most talked-about real estate developer in the country, and without as yet having put up a major structure. He estimated his personal worth at "something more than $200 million," although others claimed that this figure may have been a bit on the exuberant side. Still, for someone who had started to work full time only eight years earlier, he was doing amazingly well by any standards.

His average day found him emerging from his apartment building on East 65th Street at about 7:45 A.M. Waiting was his Cadillac limousine driven by his burly chauffeur, who did double duty as bodyguard. The limousine pulled away from the curb as Donald gave his driver the itinerary for the day. In the mornings he liked to visit his various properties and to drive past other locations he might be interested in acquiring.

His usual pattern was to make stops at his undeveloped sites first. One can almost visualize Donald driving past a vacant spread of land and finding that he could sometimes get ideas about what he wanted it to look like, say, five years down the road. He would see different possibilities arising from the thirteen-block parcel in the West 60s each time he observed it. From there he might go down to the West 30s to visit the area where his convention center would be. He could visualize the final shape of the structure, almost hear the jackhammers at work breaking up the ground. This was decompression time for him, a time for reflection and contemplation when he could let his imagination run free over the possibilities that lay ahead.

After this it was on to more mundane concerns. Perhaps he would take a run over to the project in East Orange, New Jersey, to check on building maintenance and landscaping. From there it was a quick drive to one of the Trumps' middle-income apartment complexes on Staten Island. Whenever something that he did not like caught his eye he lost no time tracking down the on-site manager to get him to correct the situation. In the late morning he directed his limousine across the Verrazano Bridge—that graceful span he knew so well—into Brooklyn. He loved to drive past the Fred C. Trump baseball field in Coney Island, then over to Trump Village and a visit with his father at the family headquarters.

By now Fred had all but turned over the major development decisions to Donald—a vote of confidence in his second son, in his skills as a negotiator, as a man with unusual vision. Donald had taken the big risk and he was coming up a winner. Fred never would have ventured across the East River if it had not been for Donald, and the Trump organization would have stayed what it was—a successful outer-borough housing developer. It was Donald who dreamed of empire, and was on the verge of turning it into reality. Fred still put in a full day's work and probably would until the day he died or became incapacitated. But Donald was now unquestionably the key decision maker in the family business.

"One of the reasons for our success," Donald said to a reporter, "was that while others were building over the last three or four years at 10 percent interest, we were buying at 5½ percent mortgages. And the units they produced in their new buildings were much smaller than the ones we were buying."

Fred knew Donald was right. The kid had not yet made a single major mistake, and you could not argue with that. To others, when his father was not present, Donald would add, "It was psychology. My father knew Brooklyn and he knew Queens very well, but now that psychology is ended." Again, "New York is either going to get much better or much worse and I'm talking about Manhattan, not the South Bronx. I don't know anything about the South Bronx."

Around noon of a typical day, Donald would say good-bye to his father and tell his driver to take him back to Manhattan. Lunch, more often than not, was at the "21" Club. Not so long ago Donald went there to look at and maybe rub shoulders with celebrities. Now, at age thirty, *he* was one of the star attractions, the waiters smiling and chattering as they escorted him to *his* table.

"Never in my life have I had a glass of alcohol or a cigarette," he would state matter-of-factly to a business associate as they sat down. According to Der Scutt this was a ploy to see if he could influence his guest's behavior. Donald admired those who stood their ground with him, as he had done with his father. Donald's tastes in food were at sharp variance with his tastes in attire. His favorite meals were more healthy than interesting. Steak medium and baked potato was a favorite; for variety, a piece of broiled fish, no sauce or butter, and a glass of ginger ale to wash it down. Other diners such as Harry Helmsley, an assortment of politicians, and businessmen made a point of coming by Donald's table to say hello.

After lunch, which he religiously kept to within an hour, it was "beaming and scheming" time. He might broker a real estate transaction for a friend, earning himself a $150,000 commission for about an hour's work, or stop in at the Chase Manhattan Bank to refinance a property his father had purchased several years earlier. With the Grand Hyatt and the convention center foremost on his mind at this time, he always tried to schedule in a visit with Der Scutt, the tall, heavyset, cigar-smoking architect on the projects.

"Donald's very demanding," Scutt laughed, discussing Donald's work habits. He was genuinely fond of the young man, admired his ability. "I was the first architect he came to. He always had his own strong ideas but he listened to me on questions of design. He thinks nothing of calling me up on a Sunday morning and saying, 'I've got an idea. See you in the office in forty minutes.' And I always go."

For public consumption Donald liked to portray himself as a happy-go-lucky bachelor dating glamorous models. "If I met the right woman I might get married," he said at the time. "But right now I have everything I want or need." Actually he had all but stopped playing the field. Ivana had become his "right woman," he was seeing her every opportunity he could and was thinking thoughts of marriage.

Once every other week or so he would fly to Los Angeles. A few years earlier he and his father had purchased land in California and more recently Donald had bought a house in Beverly Hills complete with pool and tennis courts. He said he'd made over $14 million on his California deals alone in the previous couple of years. He liked to unwind in the California sunshine, particularly when the weather began to turn damp and nasty in New York. But after a day or two in the sun, which he spent checking out new properties and working more than he played, he began to miss the frenetic pace back home and would return to New York. Ivana would fly in on Friday evenings, and he liked to be there waiting at the airport when she arrived.

27

By the end of 1976 the Trump organization comprised sixty separate partnerships and corporations and employed more than a thousand people. With Donald as its driving force the family enterprise now veered in a sharply different direction than in the days when Fred Trump was putting up semiattached houses and high-rise apartment buildings in Queens and Brooklyn. Donald viewed himself as more than merely a builder. He spoke in terms of an artistic vision of real estate development. "I love architectural creativeness," he commented in a reflective mood. "For example, the Commodore Hotel is in one of the most important locations in the city, and its reconstruction will lead to a rebirth of that area. And I like the financial creativeness too. There's a beauty in putting together a financial package that really works, whether it be through tax credits or a mortgage financing arrangement or a leaseback arrangement." He really did get misty-eyed when discussing things like mortgage financing, which tended to make most people's eyes glaze over.

"The more complicated the financing, the more Donald likes it," Der Scutt said. "If it's too simple he'll walk away from it."

Perhaps more than anything else Donald loved the gamble. He was a risk-taker who liked moving in during a recession when interest rates were tumbling. And he was smart enough to try to stack the political deck in his favor before he sat down to negotiate.

"Of course the gamble is an exciting part too," he acknowledged, smiling, "no matter how much you make out of it. You're talking about hundred-million-dollar deals where a 10 percent mistake is $10 million. But so far I've never made a bad deal."

In January of 1977 Donald put down his $250,000 deposit against the $10 million purchase price for the Commodore. He expected the financing for the cost of construction, which he estimated at $80 million, to be arranged within a couple of months. Evidently the financing he had previously lined up was beginning to unravel, and negotiations were working out to be more complicated than anticipated. The banks, at first receptive to his proposal, grew skittish because of the depressed economic climate. The success of the hotel depended to a great extent on an economic revival that would enable Donald and the Hyatt Corporation to fill the place up at an average price of $50 to $60 a room. If they could not make it work the bank's $80 million would vanish into that great terrible void called bankruptcy proceedings, and all it would have as collateral was a gutted wreck of a hotel that nobody else was interested in with or without a tax abatement. The Chase Manhattan Bank, for example, which as revealed several years later was pumping tens of millions of dollars into bankrupt countries in Africa and South America, apparently considered New York City a poorer risk than Argentina or Brazil.

But the economic upswing materialized sooner than anyone anticipated—with the possible exception of Donald Trump. Suddenly individual income started to rise and visitors came flooding into the Big Apple, driving up hotel occupancy rates. Even so it was not until the end of the year, on December 22, that Donald was able to announce, "Everything is signed."

The Bowery Savings Bank had put up $45 million and the Equitable Life Assurance Company the balance of the loan, $35 million, to solidify the deal. With all the celebrity that surrounded Donald as the *enfant terrible* of the real estate world, this was the first major project that he had actually brought to fruition. Now he was on the verge of demonstrating that he could not only build something but build one of the most talked-about structures of the time.

"I think we've proved that people still have a lot of confidence in the city," he said, obviously relieved. It had been a drawn-out ordeal for him. Elaborating on his plans for the hotel, he said for the first time that he'd actually decided to tear down the old Commodore instead of merely refurbishing it, and put up a new structure in its place. The new Grand Hyatt, said Donald, would be a true showplace, thirty-two stories high with a 170-foot-long bar enclosed within a glass facade overlooking 42nd Street, and a six-story-high atrium for a lobby. It would contain 1,407 rooms, five restaurants, a huge ballroom, several meeting rooms—and he expected it to be completed by 1980.

Patrick J. Foley, the president of Hyatt Hotels, was equally euphoric. "We're so optimistic about it," he said, "that we bought 50 percent of it from Don."

Construction of the Grand Hyatt was not the only business on Donald's agenda. His romance with Ivana had reached the critical stage. Weekend commuting was wearing out both of them. She knew well by now what he expected of a wife, and she was eager to become a vital part of his business as well. She was energetic and ambitious herself, not the type to sit home all day.

Donald and Ivana complemented each other very well. He was the wealthy scion of a self-made man who had outstripped even his father in his entrepreneurial instincts and gambits. She came from a middle-class European tradition of hard work and struggle, further tempered by growing up under a repressive political system. She had no airs about herself and was willing, anxious, to work hard in Donald's business. Their match promised to be a good one. In a quiet ceremony attended by immediate family and a few close friends, on April 9, 1977, Donald John Trump and Ivana Zelnickova Winklmayr were married at the Marble Collegiate Church on Fifth Avenue by the family's long-time minister, Dr. Norman Vincent Peale of positive-thinking fame. When reminiscing about the Trumps a few years later, Dr. Peale commented:

"I'd like to take credit for Donald but I'm not sure I'm responsible for his positive thinking. Maybe all my preaching about faith the size of a mustard seed helping to move mountains bolstered his character."

It was a busy time for Donald on other fronts as well. With family friend Mayor Beame up for reelection the controversy over the site for the New York City Convention Center degenerated into a nightmarish political quagmire. Beame faced formidable challenges in the Democratic primary from six major opponents: Bella Abzug, Herman Badillo, Mario Cuomo, Percy Sutton, Joel Harnett—all of whom were considerably to the left of the mayor and critical of his relationship with the real estate industry—and a fifty-two-year-old affable congressman named Edward Irving Koch whose positions on different issues seemed to put him simultaneously on the left, the right, and in the moderate center. Of all the contestants Koch was clearly the liveliest, blending his own special brand of skillful political commentary with a unique talent for stand-up comedy.

After four years of Abe Beame, the public was beginning to wonder if perhaps it had reacted a bit too harshly in protesting the colorful persona of the Lindsay administration. New Yorkers will forgive a great many sins, but dullness in a mayor tends not to be one of them. Koch proved to be Mayor Beame's toughest critic, as well as the wittiest, with his "three C's" slogan: "After eight years of charisma with Lindsay and four years of the clubhouse with Beame, let's try competence."

Beame further weakened his position with his handling of the convention center brouhaha. Early in his campaign he declared that he wanted to sell New York City bonds to pay for the $170 million convention center in the West 30s, and allocated $6.5 million of the city's budget to study suitable designs for the structure. The Board of Estimate opposed both of these proposals and claimed that the idea should be scrapped completely since it was becoming too expensive. Instead, the board advocated expanding the existing Coliseum Building on Columbus Circle as a better alternative.

Bella Abzug threw her prodigious hat into the ring by accusing Beame of mishandling the whole affair. She wanted the convention center built downtown in Battery Park City to avoid providing Donald Trump or any other developer with a windfall profit. Yet another candidate suggested redoing the gargantuan Central Post Office Building on 33rd Street and Eighth Avenue into a convention center. Abraham Beame responded to all this by appointing a seven-member committee to study the situation. This committee concluded that the Trump site was the best location for the center, and that city bonds should be floated to finance the project.

And so it went, round and round, until Koch emerged victorious in the Democratic primary runoff, and went on to be elected the 105th mayor of New York City on November 8 in what turned out to be a bitterly fought race. Koch, positioning himself as an independent politician beholden to no one, declared that the age of the clubhouse was over. From now on, he said, all issues would be decided on their individual merits.

Donald Trump would take note—and adjust.

28

This setback for Donald Trump in the battle over the site for the convention center was reversed a short time later with a little help from Governor Carey. During the mayoral campaign of 1977, Carey had alienated Koch by backing Mario Cuomo and suggesting to Koch that he bow out of the race and lend his support to Cuomo. After the runoff, however, when Koch had nailed down the Democratic nomination and Cuomo was restricted to the Liberal line, Carey reversed himself and supported Koch, leaving Cuomo out in left field to fend for himself. Thus was born an alliance between the new mayor and the governor of New York, with Koch not diffident about twitting his belated benefactor.

In March of 1978 Koch joined Carey in announcing their decision to locate the proposed New York City Convention Center on West 34th Street, on Donald Trump's land. Together, they advocated the sale of bonds issued by the Triborough Bridge and Tunnel Authority to raise money to build the center. According to Governor Carey this would be "the single largest economic development project in New York City's history." The total cost, they estimated, would run to $257 million.

As mentioned, what had started as a $110 million project a short time earlier had now grown to $257 million. Before the entire bungle was over, Koch and Carey would find the anticipated expenditures going as high as $450 million, with no end in sight. According to the terms of the deal, the nine-block parcel was to be sold to the Urban Development Corporation, whose condemnation authority was again required to evict unwanted tenants from the area. At this point Donald, whose out-of-pocket cost for the property was zero dollars, then brokered the sale of the land to the UDC for $12 million. He still hoped to be the developer of the project, and had gone far enough along to have Der Scutt draw up a design proposal. The sale of the parcel to the UDC was only the jumping-off point for him, but it had already earned Donald a substantial amount of money. The young baron then sat down with Peter J. Solomon, the Deputy Mayor for Economic Development, and offered to forego his broker's fee (which he said was $4.4 million) if the city and state agreed to name the project the Fred C. Trump Convention Center.

Solomon was nonplussed. Here was a man, fresh from having pulled off something of a political coup, proposing that a public facility be named after his father. Still, it was something that Solomon had to think about. The saving of a $4.4 million commission was no insignificant matter. It just might be worth going along with him:

"We thought about it and we came to the conclusion that it might be worth the $4.4 million," said Solomon. "But after about a month of knocking the idea around someone finally read the terms of the original Penn Central contract with Trump. He wasn't entitled to anything near the money he was claiming. Based on the sales price we had negotiated, his fee was only about $500,000.

"What really got me," Solomon went on, "was his bravado. It was unbelievable. He almost got us to name the convention center after his father in return for something he never really had to give away. I guess he just thought we would never read the fine print or, by the time we did, the deal to name the building after his father would have been set."

Why was it so important to Donald to have the Trump name on the center?

"Let's just say my family would deserve an honor like that," Donald said. "If it weren't for me there would be no convention center in this city." According to the terms of his agreement with Penn Central, his fee would have been higher had the site been sold for over $14 million instead of the $12 million he got for it.

The convention center controversy refused to go away or even die down. Republican Perry Duryea, gearing up for a bid to unseat Governor Carey in the 1978 election, made the subject the focal point of his campaign. He said that he was opposed to the state and city, both of which would be sharing the cost, spending more than $100 million on the center. Carey, in his attempt to win the support of upstate Republicans for the center, promised to build a football stadium in Syracuse if they went along with him. One football stadium for the upstaters in return for a $300 or $400 or $500 million convention center in Manhattan. An interesting trade-off.

In the midst of all the lobbying and arm-twisting over the financing of the convention center, with Donald in the middle of it, another ogre suddenly reared up like the Loch Ness monster from the deep. In March of 1978, with the convention center battle in full swing, the Justice Department filed a new motion in the Federal District Court in Brooklyn claiming that Trump Management had not lived up to the antidiscrimination agreement of a few years earlier. The court papers stated that Trump Management continued to discriminate against blacks even though it had agreed not to.

Roy Cohn, in his defense of Trump Management against these new charges, claimed that, "The Trumps performed so perfectly under the consent decree that expired last June that the government made no move to extend it. Today's motion is nothing more than a rehash of complaints by a couple of planted malcontents, not one of which has the slightest merit."

The attorney for the Justice Department agreed that "Trump has, in some instances, accommodated the needs of individual complainants. But it has not taken adequate action to prevent future violations."

The timing of this latest charge could not have come at a poorer time from Donald's viewpoint. With the fate of the convention center by no means resolved, in spite of the support of both Carey and Koch for his proposal, it served as a new storm cloud threatening to break over an already shaky situation.

29

Meanwhile, the setting for political theater could not have been better. It was the kind of situation Mayor Koch relished. Nobody orchestrated the media event with political impact better than he did.

On the sidewalk in front of the darkened Commodore in June 1978, Ed Koch stood grinning with a pair of scissors in his hand. Beside him stood the governor of New York, also with grin affixed. The mayor was wearing a blue hardhat with his name inscribed on the front. Behind the two, all but ignored, was the former mayor of New York City, Abraham Beame. He was the one most entitled to wear a hardhat, but he just stood there inconspicuously with a left-out-of-it-all look on his face.

"A renaissance is underway," Koch broke out in his sing-song voice, "a real renaissance in the City of New York."

Then he and Governor Carey snipped the ribbon before them, and thus was ushered in the official ground-breaking marking the demise of the old Commodore Hotel and the birth of the ultramodern Grand Hyatt. As the sound of the crowd subsided, Koch took Carey by surprise when he planted a hardhat atop the governor's boot-black hair and said into the microphone, "I forgive him. I'm supporting him for governor despite all the things he did to me."

It was vintage Ed Koch. He was backing the governor, as political reality dictated, but he was sticking a few well-placed needles in at the same time. Carey had no alternative but to stand there with the ludicrous hat on top of his head, grinning.

Following the brief speech, Ed and Hugh set off on a handshaking tour down Lexington Avenue. Koch led the way, playing the role of the host introducing the out-of-towner to his city. Carey, Brooklyn born-and-bred, could not have been enchanted by the ploy, but he was, after all, a master politician in his own right, and so threw himself into the job at hand with apparent gusto.

"Vote for him," Koch called to the crowd. "He's a terrible politician but a good governor! He saved New York City."

Ed Koch was doing what he had to do; he was supporting his governor in his own inimitable style. He was paying his dues. And Hugh Carey, surely enough, was paying his.

In the end Hugh Carey, seeking reelection, was able to convince the voters of New York State that he was the more desirable of the two major candidates. The campaign, though, was characterized by an inordinate amount of mudslinging, with each candidate accusing the other of being a tool of one or another interest group. On the roster of prime contributors to Carey's $5 million reelection campaign, Donald's generosity was second only to Hugh Carey's oilman brother. A tabulation released by the Carey campaign following the election indicated that Ed Carey had contributed $80,000 to his brother's campaign, while Donald and Fred Trump had jointly given $65,000. Real estate developer Harry Helmsley was also high up on the list with $48,000. One later estimate put the true size of these donations at nearly double the published figures.

The campaign reform law of 1974 restricted the size of outright contributions during the primary and the main campaigns, but it said nothing about money given before the primary season began. A key loophole in the law allowed backers to "lend" large sums of money, not directly to the candidate himself but rather to an intricate network of committees and support groups. In most instances these "loans" would be forgiven after Election Day or otherwise lost in a maze of complex financing arrangements. Hugh Carey, however, was able to make a sincere statement following his reelection that he could not recall an instance where he had been asked for a favor by a donor, "except that he be with us when we celebrated a victory."

Donald was now getting ready to tear down the Commodore and erect an ultramodern New York showplace that would attract visitors from around the world. It would be the kind of monumental edifice he had been dreaming about all his life.

As the demolition of the Commodore got underway, Donald hung an enormous banner bearing his name high over the facade of Grand Central Terminal, proclaiming to the world the name of the individual who was responsible for ushering in a new Golden Age for New York City. No question, no one would ever forget who he was. With the Trump banner visible throughout the midtown area, from as far away as the roof of the World Trade Center at the foot of Manhattan, from the observation deck on the Empire State Building, it was difficult not to be aware of Donald Trump. When an official from Mayor Koch's office saw the Trump name flying above Grand Central as he walked along Park Avenue, he hurried to the nearest pay phone and called Donald's office.

"My God," he said breathlessly into the telephone, "you're not tearing down Grand Central too, are you?"

Donald reassured the distraught bureaucrat that Grand Central Terminal would remain intact. He was merely restoring the facade, which was part of his agreement with the city. As he hung up the phone, one may wonder if he were not perhaps smiling.

Part Four

EMPIRE

30

Ivana Trump gave birth to their first child, a son, within a year of their marriage. At age thirty-one Donald now had an heir, inevitably named Donald John Trump, Jr.

The first year of marriage for Donald and Ivana was a whirlwind of meetings, negotiations, megadeals, and nonstop activity. Previously Ivana had been in Donald's company mostly on weekends. Weekends for Donald represented a week's work for most anyone else, so Ivana had some idea of what she was getting into. Even on Saturday nights Donald was hardly able to get through a meal without interrupting it with half a dozen phone calls. But the frenzied pace of his weekday schedule was enough to give ordinary humans a nervous breakdown, and Ivana had to shift her neurological system into overdrive to keep up with him.

"I wanted a man who was dominant," she reminisced later on,

"someone who was very successful in business, someone I could respect. When I first married Donald it was very rough that first year. I got pregnant, I quit my job in Montreal, totally gave up my modeling career, and every day in New York Donald was introducing me to about a thousand people. I didn't think I would be able to take it." She was not the type to spend her time at afternoon teas with her friends, assuming the lifestyle of a Park Avenue society matron, but Donald's demanding pace was still more than she had bargained for.

For his part Donald was proud of Ivaska (his nickname for Ivana), eager to show her off to his friends and business associates, and in his fashion had a tendency on occasion to refer to her as Canada's "top model." Still, the first-year wrinkles in their marriage were relatively minor, and basically they were off to a good running start. Ivana definitely had found herself a dominant husband who was successful in business, and Donald had a wife who was beautiful, intelligent, and nearly as competitive as he was.

The Trump fortunes were healthier now than ever before. Donald had gambled big on Manhattan and had come up a winner, thanks to his own brilliance, inventiveness, and the political leverage he enjoyed. His modus operandi was to take in a partner who agreed to put up the risk money in return for a percentage of the deal. Unlike other developers who preceded him he did not believe in syndicating his projects among a multitude of limited partners. Donald called the tune properly in New York City. His timing was impeccable, and he was in a position to reap a great fortune because of it.

"I either had the insight or the foolishness to take everything and invest it in Manhattan in 1975. The city was a disaster and it was supposed to get worse," he recalled, analyzing his situation a few years later. "The time that New York started taking off was literally the day I started to build the Grand Hyatt. So I owned all this property all over Manhattan and, with the leverage situation, six months later it became worth twice what I paid. Then it became worth five times. All of a sudden this property goes up and up in value."

But Donald was not finished gambling on Manhattan; his well-timed moves gave him the confidence to pyramid his fortune. In January 1979 he announced that he was negotiating another extremely complicated deal to buy the building on the east side of Fifth Avenue between 56th and 57th streets that housed Bonwit Teller, the forty-nine-year-old specialty store. The once-fashionable store had been losing money all through the years of the recession, and the parent company that owned it, Genesco, Inc., of Nashville, Tennessee, was desperately in need of cash.

The exact terms of the purchase were not immediately available, but the price was said to be in the range of $10 million to $24 million, depending on Donald's ability to obtain the kind of zoning changes he wanted. Complicating the whole arrangement was the fact that the building and the 20,000-square-foot lot on which Bonwit Teller stood was owned by the Equitable Life Assurance Company, and it was by no means certain that Equitable was in a mood to sell. In addition, the building adjoining the Bonwit Teller site was owned and occupied by Tiffany & Company, the chic jewelry concern. Since Donald's plans included demolishing the old structure and putting up a mammoth high-rise containing boutiques, offices, and condominiums, he would somehow have to negotiate for the air rights above Tiffany's to put it all together.

It was an extremely complicated package deal involving negotiations over a building, land, and air rights with three separate owners. It was, in short, the kind of situation Donald loved best and was so good at. In this particular instance he was putting into action his entire philosophy of real estate: "If you go to Paris, if you go to Duluth, the best location is called the Tiffany location." What could be better than building directly next to Tiffany's, *surrounding* Tiffany's, as it were?

"I set out to get the true Tiffany location—the location right next door to Tiffany's," he said. "The location is probably the most prestigious address in New York."

By Donald's own admission, the first time he contacted Genesco about the purchase of Bonwit Teller "they literally laughed at me." After a bit of detective work, however, he discovered that Genesco had twenty-nine years remaining on its lease with Equitable, and it was starved for cash. Bonwit represented a constant drain on the company's cash flow. Donald called again and again, knowing he was dealing from a position of strength, and offered to buy out Genesco's lease for $10 million. Finally, Genesco decided to accept the offer.

"Donald has the uncanny ability to smell blood in the water," a spokesman for Genesco acknowledged. For the Tennessee concern, Bonwit represented, so to speak, the corporate equivalent of Custer's Last Stand.

"Donald Trump can smell a good deal," Roy Cohn agreed, "even when it looks dismal to everybody else."

"If it is not impossible Donald is simply not interested," Louise Sunshine concurred. "There has to be creativity. Money ceased to be the object some time ago."

Stage one of the complex negotiation was now in place. Stage two required dealing with Tiffany, as well, of course, as the city. To do what he wanted to do on the site, he had to get approval for a package of zoning changes and tax abatements to make the numbers come out right. In February, less than two weeks after his first announcement, Donald obtained 100,000 square feet of air rights above Tiffany's for $5 million. Tiffany retained a portion just above its building, enough to allow it to add on another three stories just before Donald started to build.

But there was still Equitable to contend with, and this company was not exactly hungry for cash. The giant insurance conglomerate had come up with $35 million not too long ago to help him finance the construction of the Grand Hyatt.

"We were watching Trump to see if he could put it all together," said George Peabody, senior vice-president for real estate at Equitable. "To tell the truth, he surprised us. We were kind of skeptical at first, but everything Donald promised to get done, he did. He really knows how to make things happen in New York."

In the end, Equitable decided to go along with Donald on this deal as it had on the Grand Hyatt. The company sold him the building and the 20,000-square-foot lot for a 50 percent partnership in his project, and no money down. It was another display of financial wizardry, some might say razzle-dazzle, for Donald Trump.

31

The higher Donald's star of fortune rose, the lower his older brother
Fred's seemed to be sinking. Fred had hoped that a change of direction,
working on charter boats in the Florida waters, would somehow repair
his damaged psyche, give his life a new sense of purpose. Not so.
Fred, according to a family associate, hit bottom and had to be rescued.
Divorced now from his wife Linda, he returned to the family enclave
in Jamaica Estates to live with his parents.

His father, sympathetic to his plight, tried to handle the situation
with delicacy. But his oldest son's predicament seemed beyond his
comprehension. For the life of him, he couldn't understand such a turn
of events. Hadn't he preached all his life that with hard work and
determination everyone could make it in the end? And now the condition of his firstborn son was threatening to undermine his whole
system of beliefs.

Young Fred's action belied the old notion of Thomas Wolfe that you can't go home again. You can, but not necessarily under even tolerable circumstances.

Against all odds Donald was putting it all together. No deal, apparently, was too complicated for his talents. He welcomed the challenge and considered the details of an intricate negotiation as a kind of higher art form.

"I love real estate [because] there's something about creating something that's visible. There's an artistic merit," he said.

In March 1979 he had discussed his plans to tear down the old Bonwit Teller building and erect in its place a $100 million, sixty-eight-story skyscraper (later reduced to fifty-eight stories) of bronze-colored glass containing retail boutiques and stores, offices, and condominiums. He hoped to begin demolition soon, start construction by January 1980, and complete the project within two and half years. He anticipated building a 100-foot-long corridor leading into the building from Fifth Avenue, opening into a five-story-high atrium filled with retail space, elevators, escalators, landscaped terraces, and a cascading waterfall. Above this would be thirteen stories of offices and forty more of condominiums. The firm of Poor, Swanke, Hayden & Connell would design the structure, with his old buddy Der Scutt as the partner in charge of the project. To do all this Donald still required the approval of the City Planning Commission, Manhattan Community Board 5, and the Board of Estimate. Representing his case before the various city agencies was Samuel H. Lindenbaum, the son of his father's old lawyer and political sidekick.

It was at this time that Donald confirmed the final details of perhaps his most complicated deal to date. Genesco was to be paid $10 million for the remainder of its lease with Equitable; the insurance company would turn over the building and land to the Trump organization in return for a 50 percent partnership; and Tiffany & Company was selling 100,000 square feet of air rights above its own building for $5 million.

Everything was set except the zoning variances needed to put up the structure, and a package of tax abatements. Once again the opposition sharpened its knives and prepared for a knock-down, drag-out fight with Donald Trump.

"I'm worried about the bulk of another tall building in the area," said Hal Negbur, the chairman of Community Board 5. "I suggest a six-month moratorium on new buildings to study the impact of density. We ought to stop and think before we get such a congested area that we ruin it."

"The basic point is," said Robert F. Wagner, Jr., now the chairman of the City Planning Commission, "it is a very significant site and we want to take a careful look at the building."

Donald responded by asking a loaded question. "Do you want Bonwit Teller to come back to Fifth Avenue? It's as simple as this: if I don't get a zone change, I don't rent to Bonwit's."

The question of the tax abatement was also heating up. Donald filed for an abatement under Section 421-A, and was originally turned down on the grounds that the law was intended to encourage the construction of low- and middle-income housing on "underutilized land" and his proposal did not fit within these guidelines. Enter Roy Cohn to take up the gauntlet for Donald. After winning the first round, the city took its case to the Court of Appeals. Manhattan Borough President Andrew Stein, whom the Trumps had supported in various campaigns, arranged a meeting between Donald and Anthony Gliedman, the city's Commissioner for Housing Preservation and Development. Trump stated his case to Gliedman; the commissioner apparently remained unconvinced. He knew the Trumps from their involvement with the Madison Club in Brooklyn, and Donald felt that he was being singled out for unfair treatment. According to Gliedman, as recounted in Ed Koch's

Mayor, Donald called him at home the same evening and said:

"I don't know whether it's still possible for you to change your decision or not, but I want you to know that I am a very rich and powerful person in this town and there is a reason I got that way. I will never forget what you did."

The tax abatement in question was not in the same league as the one Donald received for the Grand Hyatt, but it was substantial enough in its own right. It would mean a savings of about $40 million to the Trump organization over a ten-year period. After receiving Donald's phone call, Gliedman turned to Mayor Koch, who had little alternative but to back him up, though Koch says he did it out of loyalty to Gliedman. In any event, details of the incident were already getting out, and Koch was sensitive to any appearance of being beholden to anyone. Donald went back to court and launched a new offensive, not only against the city for refusing to grant him the same abatement it routinely gave other developers, but also against Anthony Gliedman personally for "discriminating" against him. His claim against the city was for $138 million in damages, and his claim against Gliedman was for $10 million.

"This automatic tax abatement," Donald said in the tone of a man who truly felt he had been wronged, "that everybody else had gotten before me, and is all ready to be signed, all of a sudden gets rejected."

Gliedman's interpretation of events, naturally enough, was markedly different from Donald's. His position was that Fifth Avenue in midtown did not qualify as "underutilized land" by any reasonable definition. Donald pressed his case forward and five years later was vindicated. After a series of court decisions that saw the city and the Trump organization winning alternate rounds, his abatement was finally granted by New York State's highest court, the Court of Appeals, early in 1984. The court ruled that the failing condition of the building at the time of Donald's original request did qualify as "underutilized land."

In spite of this victory, however, Donald refused to drop his cases against the city and the commissioner, and they were still pending in federal court at the end of 1984.

Donald did get the zoning variances he wanted on the site, which gave him the green light to go ahead and put his monumental plan in action. It was an indication of how badly he wanted to put up this building that he was willing to proceed before the issue of the tax abatement was fully resolved. This, after all, was going to be the fulfillment of a lifelong dream. He was going to create one of the most talked-about superstructures of modern times, and he was going to call it Trump Tower.

Before construction got underway, however, a new snag surfaced that once again threatened to undermine the whole project. Councilman Henry Stern, still fuming over the Grand Hyatt tax abatement as well as Donald's role in the convention center fiasco, tried to derail the agreement that had been worked out between the Trump organization and the three city agencies that had already approved the zoning changes. After intense lobbying on his part, the city asked Donald to sit down once again and consider a small compromise on the deal. The final design for Trump Tower called for the construction of a fifty-eight-story tower of dark mirror-glass with a stepladder effect on the front and sides that provided the building with twenty-eight separate facets.

According to Der Scutt, Donald's own father had said to him after viewing the architect's rendering, "We've been putting up buildings with four sides all over Queens and Brooklyn, and here you're planning to build one with twenty-eight sides in Manhattan."

"It's important," Donald replied to his father. "These are luxury condominiums and the building is designed so that every apartment has two different views over the city."

Henry Stern, troubled that Trump Tower was not in the tradition of the existing architecture on Fifth Avenue, lobbied for a masonry facade more in keeping with the historical look of the area. In the end, Donald was allowed to go ahead with his original concept, but the compromise limited his building to fifty-eight stories instead of his intended sixty-eight.

In his fashion, Donald in effect managed to overturn even this relatively minor defeat later on. He simply said that Trump Tower was sixty-eight stories high, and so it was reported in the press. Donald may have assumed, accurately, that nobody was likely to take the trouble to stand out on Fifth Avenue and count all the way up.

32

Councilman Henry J. Stern decided to do battle with Donald Trump on another issue at this time. In April 1979, with the Grand Hyatt under construction and Trump Tower about to become a reality, Stern uncovered an issue involving Donald that raised his blood to a steady boil. This one concerned the Vanderbilt Tennis Club near Grand Central Terminal.

The facility was owned by the Metropolitan Transportation Authority, the same venerable institution that operated the subway system. When the lease for the tennis club expired that year, the MTA was approached by a former top-ranked player named Hamilton Richardson who wanted to take over the club and run it himself. He offered the MTA an annual rent of $100,000, renewable in five years, plus 10 percent of the gross revenues above $200,000 a year. The MTA studied the proposal, then turned around and offered a twenty-year lease to

Donald Trump for $80,000 a year in rent, eventually rising to $95,000 annually by the time the lease expired. According to the terms of its deal with Donald, the MTA would not receive a percentage of the club's revenues.

This arrangement struck Stern and other observers as somewhat curious. Why would the MTA turn down Hamilton Richardson for a less lucrative deal with Donald Trump? It did not seem to make any sense, and Stern attempted to block it. The councilman claimed that Donald Trump had once again negotiated a "sweetheart contract" through his political connections.

Donald had a different interpretation of the situation: "The MTA wanted someone who could make a big investment to repair and maintain those courts. By giving me the contract they knew they had someone who had the assets to do just that. It was no political favor."

Stern's position was that the MTA had given away too much in return for Donald's commitment to upgrade the facilities, that it would be cheaper in the long run to go along with Richardson's terms. So the controversy dragged on for almost a year with little or nothing being done to resolve it. In February 1980 Stern brought the issue to the attention of Edward V. Regan, the comptroller of New York State. At Stern's request, Regan contacted all parties involved and asked them to renegotiate the lease. Regan, no great friend of Governor Carey, used the opportunity to publicize Louise Sunshine's role in the affair. Louise, according to Regan, had recently been appointed by Carey to a $17,000-a-year job with the New York State Thruway Authority while she was simultaneously earning some $100,000 a year with the Trump organization.

But Donald was adamantly against reopening negotiations. "We've spent close to $150,000 and have the most beautiful tennis center in the world," he said. "I wouldn't make a tremendous investment without a lease that allows me to make my money back." The next day Donald reiterated his position and said that he would not redo the terms of the lease unless he were reimbursed the $250,000 he had already spent on rehabilitating the courts. No one seemed to pick up on the disparity between the two figures.

Hamilton Richardson, reached on the telephone in Dallas for his assessment of what had happened, said: "I can't understand how they justified doing it."

Richard Ravitch, the chairman of the MTA, did not help Stern's case when he was called upon to renegotiate the lease with Donald Trump. He admitted to being annoyed that the councilman was making such a fuss over "a couple of dollars" at a time when the MTA had to deal with its $200 million deficit. Everybody in the city was screaming about preserving the fifty-cent subway fare, and he had more important things to worry about than a lease on a tennis club.

As it turned out, Stern was whipping a dead horse. The lease had already been signed by both parties, neither of which had any interest in changing its terms. It was a *fait accompli*.

If Donald wanted a wife who would pitch in and help out with his business, one who did not mind getting her Charles Jourdan pumps a bit muddy at the construction sites, Ivana was tailor-made. She plunged into the construction of the Grand Hyatt, visiting the grimy pit every day, supervising the electricians, plumbers, carpenters, and steel-workers to such a degree that she could state with considerable reason later on that she knew "every nail in the hotel." Mostly interested in the design and decorations, she selected the pink-hued Paradiso marble that went into the lobby and presided over the installment of the walnut paneling, the bronze columns, gold handrails, golden brown velours, zig-zagging metalwork hanging from the ceiling, the multilevel water-fall—in short, the very look and feel of the hotel that turned it into a gawker's paradise. Ivana had an eye for the ultramodern in fashion that complemented, or perhaps reinforced, her husband's taste.

"This is the way I help Donald," Ivana said with her Austro-Czech accent that turned "w's" into "v's" and "th's" into "z's." She checked to make sure the water didn't burble in the waterfall. "All the details to worry about. If I can do these little things he knows he can trust me totally and then he can spend his time on the more important things."

The foremen and workers on the job attested to the fact that Ivana was a taskmaster as she made her way past mounds of rubble and roaring machinery. "When will it be finished?" she would ask. "When can I tell Donald the job will be done?" An electrician who failed to show up one day because he was busy elsewhere was singled out for special treatment.

"After she leaves I always have a thousand new things to do," he said glumly. "You can never satisfy Mrs. Trump."

"I have to put on this tough act," she said after leaving for the day, "because if you say please, please to these guys, the job will never get done the way we want it done."

While Ivana made the Grand Hyatt her overriding concern, Donald moved quickly to iron out the final details before starting work on Trump Tower. In July of 1979 he announced that he was negotiating with the Allied Stores Corporation, which was the owner of all the other Bonwit Teller locations except the one on Fifth Avenue, to open a new Bonwit's in Trump Tower. The new Bonwit Teller would occupy considerably less space than it had in the old ten-story structure— 80,000 square feet instead of the original 200,000. By September the details of the lease with Allied were agreed on. Allied would pay the Trump organization $2.5 million a year over a twenty-five-year period for four floors in the new tower. Donald called the terms a "giveaway" for Allied, an accurate enough statement since the rent came to a little more than $30 a square foot in a building that would eventually command many times that amount for retail space. Thomas Macloce, Allied's president, was pleased enough with the lease that he promised to make "a substantial investment in the Bonwit store."

In the days remaining before actual construction began on Trump Tower an unfortunate incident occurred that reminds one that the past is always with us, even if dormant for the moment. Donald was about to achieve the goal of his lifetime, the creation of a dramatic superstructure on Fifth Avenue that would bear his name, when a demon from the past returned to haunt him.

In July 1979 a young black woman claimed that she visited a real estate broker in Brooklyn and told him that she wanted to buy a house in a good residential neighborhood, preferably in the Midwood, Marine Park, or Sheepshead Bay sections of the borough. The realtor, as reported by *The New York Times* July 29, 1979, looked her in the eye and told her, "I'm sorry, but I think that in any of those neighborhoods you'd feel like a black marble in a bowl of vanilla ice cream."

The remark was evidently intended to lay out in humorous fashion an unpleasant fact of life, but the lady was not amused. She also happened to be an investigator for the city's Human Rights Commission, checking on reports that real estate agents were "steering" blacks and other minorities away from white neighborhoods. According to her report two of the firms responsible for this practice were the Lefrak Organization and Trump Management. Donald was given the opportunity to express his own feelings on the subject.

The use of decoys, he said, "was a form of horrible harassment. As far as we're concerned the case against us is just not valid. We don't practice any race discrimination."

162

33

"Galanos—I just ordered eight pieces from him," said Ivana Trump. "Then I like Valentino and Chloe for evening and, for after ski, Kamali. But I don't like Saint Laurent. For shoes, Charles Jourdan. They make a fortune off me."

Ivana, at age thirty, was stunning as ever, tailored to perfection. Her golden hair was parted in the middle and ironed flat so that it hung down in an unbroken free-fall below her shoulders.

She said that Donald wears clothing designed by Pierre Cardin, as well as by Bill Blass and Saint Laurent. Twice a year, "when he's in a very good mood," he goes to Barney's and buys ten or fifteen new suits. Missing from Donald's wardrobe these days were his old plum-colored suits with matching shoes. Ivana, deferential to her husband in most other areas, usually got her way as far as fashion was concerned. This was her province, and Donald trusted her instincts when it came to clothing and design. Lately, Donald had taken to appearing in conservative dark suits and ties and thin-soled loafers with tassels on the instep. Except for his relative youth and flamboyant manner, he fitted the image of other well-heeled businessmen about town.

The Trumps' home, after just over two years of marriage, was a spacious eight-room apartment on Fifth Avenue with a magnificent view of Central Park. It had an enormous entrance hall, a solarium between the dining room and the kitchen, and an entertainment center that Ivana referred to as the "galleria."

"I wanted a very dramatic galleria," she explained, "so I put in dark marble floors with little lights around the mirrors like a waterfall." A coffee table was made entirely of real bone from Casa Bella in Italy, and the dining-room tables were cloaked in goatskin. Stretched between two large windows overlooking Central Park was a hammock, and the living room was done in beige wall-to-wall deep-piled carpeting that blended with the beige velvet upholstery of the furniture.

Life in the city was a maelstrom of business and social activity for Donald and Ivana. "My life is one big negotiation," he said. Ivana usually got up around eight o'clock, had a grapefruit for breakfast. During construction of the Grand Hyatt she made a point of visiting the building site each day to make certain the demanding schedule was being adhered to. Getting it ready on time was her major enterprise. Three times a week she made time for vigorous exercise classes, and twice a week she visited her hairdresser. Most days she made sure she was back home by four when her masseuse arrived.

"I have to look pretty and fresh because we have to entertain people so much," she said reasonably enough.

Evenings in the city were mostly taken up with one social event or another. Several times a week they had dinner out, at "21," Chantilly, Le Cirque, or the Czech Pavilion, presumably Ivana's favorite. When they ate at home Ivana did the cooking, a passion of hers.

Donald was the "all-American boy" and he preferred steak and potatoes to anything called "cuisine. I was making all kinds of beautiful sauces but I finally gave up," she said.

After dinner, whether at home or at a restaurant, they invariably had something to do and some place to go. If they did not visit Le Club, Regine's, Doubles, Studio 54, or some such, they attended a Broadway play or perhaps a sporting event at Madison Square Garden, which Ivana enjoyed as much as Donald. Ivana also devoted time and money to several charities, and was especially active with the United Cerebral Palsy Association.

To get away from it all when they felt a need for a break they limoed out to their summer home in Wainscott, Long Island, or flew to their ski house in Aspen for a weekend of skiing. According to Ivana, they deliberately kept their lives low-key when they were unwinding, eating simply at home and retiring early.

"We don't give our phone number to many people," she said. "We don't give parties and we accept invitations only from very close friends."

All in all, they lived the life of the very rich who were becoming increasingly socially prominent thanks to Donald's growing fame and success. With all the glamor and sparkle that characterized their existence, however, there was one corner that was downright mundane, that stripped away the veneer and added a human dimension. Once a week, like any dutiful middle-class couple from Queens or Main Street, U.S.A., they trekked out to Jamaica Estates for the family dinner with Donald's parents.

Some things, good things it seemed, never changed for the Trump family, no matter how great the success.

34

By the beginning of 1980 Donald Trump was about to achieve his ambition to become the new William Zeckendorf. Certainly he was the most controversial real estate baron of his time, the creator of the most dramatic new structures being built anywhere in the country, perhaps the world. He was a showman, a nonpareil negotiator, and a financial genius who thrived on complexity.

Part of his success was due to his ability to walk away from the deals that looked as though they would not get off the ground. The convention center had gotten away from him—indeed, had gotten away from everyone involved with it. Latest estimates on its construction cost were in the vicinity of $500 million. It appeared as though it might never be built. Donald, however, had come out all right. He had gotten the city and state to agree to build the center on his land, then made money on the transfer of the site to the UDC. More recently he was negotiating for the right to put up a twin-tower hotel adjoining the convention center should it ever become a reality.

His decision to abandon his plans for luxury apartments on the thirteen-block parcel on the westside had also been a smart one. This project became bogged down because of dissenting community groups and the insistence by the city that public facilities in the area be upgraded before any construction could begin. Donald had allowed his options to expire, and the site was acquired instead by an Argentine businessman named Francisco Macri and a New York City parking garage mogul named Abraham Hirschfeld. They immediately announced their intention to build a billion-dollar complex called Lincoln West, a plan which quickly became entangled in a maze of political and economic problems. (In 1984, when it was clear that Macri and Hirschfeld would never get their plan off the drawing board, Donald seized the opportunity to bail them out of the mess and renegotiate the deal with the city.)

Donald Trump had so far made all the right moves. He was going ahead with deals that worked, and had sidestepped the ones that did not. Many of his critics were waiting for him to fall on his face, but he was demonstrating a remarkable ability to stay on his feet.

Now he was ready to turn his vision into reality. In March 1980 the way was cleared for him to raze the Bonwit Teller building, a structure that typified for many the kind of masonry-facade, art deco architecture that gave Fifth Avenue its unique look. Unfortunately, it was little more than a museum piece now and no longer economically viable. There was, though, a sense of history in the building's carved surface, a sense of time and place and a long-gone past. Many felt it belonged on Fifth Avenue, as, for example, did the Scribner building and bookstore nine blocks to the south.

Directly above the entrance to the Bonwit Teller building was an ornate grillwork of interlocking geometric designs that measured twenty feet high by thirty feet long. The grillwork was made of Benedict nickel, silver in color when it was new in 1930 but tarnished over the years until it had taken on the look of bronze. It was designed by Otto J. Teegen, an architect who was employed by the firm of Ely Jacques Kahn. High up on the facade of the building, between the eighth and ninth floors, were two fifteen-foot-high bas relief stone sculptures in the art deco style. The limestone sculptures were done in two panels and set into a bed of concrete and steel, depicting partially draped female nudes. Before beginning the million-dollar demolition, both the grillwork and the two sculptures were promised by Donald to the Metropolitan Museum of Art on condition that it was "economically viable to remove them intact."

To do so, scaffolding had to be built beneath the sculptures and the cement walls had to be carved away from the panels with a carborundum saw, then collapsed inside the building. The bas reliefs would then have to be braced to keep them upright and moved onto specially built platforms where they would be crated and lowered with cranes to the street. The cost of removal was estimated at about $32,000. It was a delicate surgical operation, to be sure, but the only way possible of preserving the panels.

"The reliefs are as important pieces of art deco as the sculptures on the Rockefeller building," said Robert Miller, a Fifth Avenue art dealer who appraised the sculptures' monetary value at "several hundreds of thousands of dollars."

As demolition began in March, great care had to be taken not to damage the Tiffany building on the corner of 57th Street. Instead of the usual iron-ball and dynamite techniques used in demolition projects, Bonwit Teller had to be "imploded" so that the structure collapsed inwardly instead of exploding onto the street. The building was stripped internally first, debris dropped down elevator shafts to be removed later. To his pleasant surprise, Donald discovered much of value in the old store that he was able to salvage and sell as scrap for "a few hundred thousand dollars." The market at the time brought him seventy cents a pound for brass and copper pipes, twenty cents a pound for steel. The heavy steel girders used in the original construction sold for a few thousand dollars apiece.

By June the once-lush interior of the fifty-year-old department store was a melange of torn carpeting, tangled Venetian blinds, scattered bricks, broken sheetrock, shattered tile, and twisted wiring. Much of the work was done at night under glaring lights to avoid injuring pedestrians on the sidewalk out front. Finally it was time to remove the grillwork over the entrance and the sculptures high up on the facade. The surgery was about to begin.

35

Even the best laid plans of Donald Trump could, to paraphrase the poet, go astray. In June the crew foreman on the Bonwit Teller job informed him that the removal of the art deco sculptures and the grillwork was going to result in a longer than expected delay. There was no way the surgery could be performed quickly.

"How long a delay are you talking about?" Donald asked.

"Two weeks, maybe three," was the reply.

According to an account in *New York Magazine* Donald blew up and gave the order to forget the surgery and go forward. Besides, he'd promised to salvage the grillwork and sculpture only so long as it was economically feasible to do so. He couldn't, he apparently decided, let the baby drown in a salvage job.

Peter M. Warner, a tenant in the building across the street from Bonwit's, looked on as the demolition was taking place. For years he had glanced out his window in the course of the day, admiring the old structure and, particularly, the bas relief sculptures directly across from his own office. On Thursday, June 5, 1980, he saw something take place that deeply upset him.

"I really couldn't believe my eyes," he said. "I looked out the window and saw that they had cut the left-hand panel in half horizontally and were proceeding to do the same to the right-hand panel."

The destruction of the sculptures was done with jackhammers. The workmen pounded them until they split in half in order to loosen them from their beds. When they were freed from their resting places they were pulled loose with crowbars and pushed inside the structure, where they fell and shattered.

The uproar that followed lasted for weeks. At first Donald refused to talk to anyone about the incident, referring questions instead to John Baron, one of his vice-presidents. His spokesman, however, only provoked further public indignation with his comment that "the merit of the stones was not great enough to justify the effort to save them. They were without artistic merit." Builders should perhaps not be critics, at least where self-interest seems so linked to preservation disputes. In any case, Baron said that an independent appraisal had determined that the sculptures were worth only about $7,000 in an auction. Which, to critics, was not the point. When asked to respond, Ashton Hawkins, vice-president of the Board of Trustees of the Met, said:

"How extraordinary. Can you imagine the museum accepting them if they were not of artistic merit? Architectural sculpture of this quality is rare and would have made definite sense in our collections. Their monetary value was not what we were interested in."

Robert Miller, the Fifth Avenue art dealer, agreed with Ashton. "They were very much in the art deco style," he said, "very beautiful and very gracious. They'll never be made again."

Donald's own architect, Der Scutt, described the panels as "magnificent things." He had originally wanted to incorporate them into the new building but was overruled by Donald, who, Der Scutt said, wanted a "more contemporary design." Well, they certainly weren't contemporary.

Donald clearly did not anticipate the furor that resulted from his decision, and subsequently said that he was sorry he didn't take the extra time to preserve the panels. But, at minimum, a public relations damage had already been done, and he tried to put a better face on it. Safety first:

"My biggest concern was the safety of the people in the street below. If one of those stones had slipped, people could have been killed. To me it would not have been worth that kind of risk."

The problem with this reasoning was that much of the demolition work was being done at night to avoid just the sort of accident Donald was talking about. But it was true that the $32,000 cost of removal, a relatively minor sum to Donald, was not his main objection. The crucial element, aside from his desire to get the buildings opened on time, was the tremendous amount of money a three-week delay would have cost him. Such a delay in a major construction piles up expenses not unlike a similar delay on a big motion picture. By his calculation he would have been faced with an additional $150,000 in real estate taxes, $250,000 in extra interest payments plus $100,000 to $200,000 in lost revenues because of a later opening—a total of over $500,000. While his critics zeroed in on the $32,000 figure and lambasted him for being tight-fisted, he was actually, and not unreasonably, concerned about the extra half-million dollars it would have cost to remove the sculptures intact.

If the uproar over the shattered panels was not enough to keep him occupied, in the midst of it all someone noticed that the grillwork over the entranceway was missing. It had evidently been overlooked in the indignant outbursts over the sculptures. Now the spotlight shifted once again. And once again Donald assigned the job of fielding questions about the grillwork to John Baron.

"We don't know what happened to it," said Baron.

This statement turned out to be no more acceptable than his comment about the merit of the panels. Otto J. Teegen, the architect who had designed the grillwork fifty years earlier, said that the grillwork was enormous. "It's not a thing you could slip in your coat pocket and walk away with." In the commotion that followed it was learned that the grillwork, too, would have been difficult to remove in one piece. It was cut up and sold for the scrap value of its metal content along with the twisted brass pipes and metal wiring that had been salvaged from inside the store.

Donald, of course, would have preferred that none of this had ever happened. In erecting the building of his dreams he had, unhappily, stirred up a hornet's nest. He regarded himself—and not unreasonably—as an artist of sorts in his own right, and now *The New York Times* was accusing him of "aesthetic vandalism" and others were calling him an "unenlightened developer." It was not in keeping with the desired image or intent.

Still, as Emerson reasoned, life has built-in compensations.

36

The day after the story about the sculptures hit the newspapers I must've gotten two dozen calls from people who wanted apartments in Trump Tower when it's finished. It was fantastic promotion. Only the very best people can afford it," said Donald. "They'll be the highest prices ever paid by man. King Khalid of Saudi Arabia has asked about one entire floor at $11 million. Sophia Loren is looking at one of the apartments at $1.8 million. And the retail outlets will be rented for the highest prices ever paid for Fifth Avenue real estate, literally twice as high as anyone has ever gotten."

The controversy triggered over the art deco panels turned into a Trump bonanza. People all over the world were made aware of the soaring monolith going up on one of the world's most famed avenues. It was in part a measure of his incredible good fortune that even an event that generated so much negative publicity ended up benefiting him. It seemed Donald Trump could do no wrong. He was, as they say, on a roll, on a hot streak, in which every move created headlines that were rapidly turning his name into a household word. The Chase Manhattan Bank had recently come across with a $100 million construction loan to guarantee the project. The Bowery Bank and Equitable were financing the Grand Hyatt. He was, indeed, New York's newest Golden Boy—and everybody wanted to be his partner.

"I've had to make my deals with a certain amount of flash," said Donald. "I want materials that glitter, that sparkle, the best of everything, you understand."

The architects who worked with him tried to rein him in some and get him to adopt a more conventional style. "Donald sometimes is a bit naive," said Der Scutt. "He has his own very clean, modern tastes, and he's not interested in what's old."

Philip Johnson, another prominent architect who later suggested that Donald build a modern-day castle on Madison Avenue, said, "His taste is all right, but it is sometimes overwhelmed by his sense of publicity. He'll become less and less glitzy."

"If the charge is that Donald is unsophisticated," commented Roy Cohn, "it is in some ways right. If you go with Donald to see an art collection, he's not that interested. He'd rather look out the windows at buildings."

"If that's not art," Donald said, referring to his preferred kind of structures, "I don't know what is."

The point was, Donald did see art in the sleek, soaring, multifaceted structures he was building. Efforts by his architects and others to get him to incorporate more traditional forms in his structures went against his grain. And the public, apparently, agreed with him. Whether one liked what he was doing or not, he seemed to know instinctively what people wanted. His buildings, when completed, drew crowds. They worked economically. Some might say he was concretizing the tastes and values of mass-market television programs. He was and is perhaps more closely in touch with the tastes of his time, for better or for worse according to one's preferences, than any other developer on the scene. His dim view of the Bonwit Teller sculptures came from his gut. It was his way of rebelling against, of answering, those who criticized so vehemently his own tastes and view of structural art.

With the Grand Hyatt scheduled to open in a matter of weeks and construction of Trump Tower ready to begin, Donald was already contemplating a dozen new projects on his drawing board. He stared down with a proprietary interest at a $35,000 architectural model of midtown Manhattan in the center of his office. All the major skyscrapers were carefully re-created in balsa wood—the AT&T building, IBM, GM, Bergdorf Goodman, Tiffany. But the scale model of Trump Tower stood in the midst of them in glittering bronze glass, outshining all the others.

"What a box, I hate it," Donald said to one of his architects, referring to the GM building. "It overpowers Trump Tower. Let's get rid of it."

"But, Mr. Trump," replied architect Maloof, "we need it to show the scope. I don't think you can get rid of the GM builidng."

"What do *you* think?" he asked Maloof, "am I right? Should I get rid of GM?"

"Don't worry, Mr. Trump," he answered diplomatically, "your building will stand out."

One thing that had been bothering Donald was Ivana's desire to make Trump Tower an all-electric building. Ever since she was a small girl, she told the author, she had been frightened of gas. Donald's architects, however, told him that gas was more upper class.

"People who appreciate food will insist on gas stoves," said Der Scutt, the point being that presumably more subtle cooking could result from the more controllable gradations of heat from gas burners.

On this issue Donald would not give in to his wife. Gas was more upscale; all-electric was considered middle class. "Tell Ivaska to stay out of this," he said with finality. And that was the end of that.

"Trump Tower will be the greatest building in New York," Donald said with conviction. "There will never be another skyscraper built like it. Because of me they've changed the midtown zoning. And it's kind of sad because there is nothing I can do that will be greater after this."

Then, as in a flash, he was off to the adjoining room to check on the market. Donald had started investing in precious metals, and was in early on the spectacular move that saw gold run from $35 to over $800 an ounce in a relatively short time. By the time the rush was over he would walk away from this venture with a profit of more than $30 million.

After his phone calls, project planning, and paper shuffling were over for the day, it was time to visit his architects. Donald did not believe in calling ahead to announce himself.

"I like to surprise these guys and see if I can catch them not working on my project when I know and *they* know that all their time must be spent on Trump Tower," he said.

Well, he was obsessed with the results; why shouldn't those he retained be likewise?

The big night arrived on Thursday, September 5, 1980. Everyone was there for the grand opening of the Grand Hyatt—Governor Carey, Mayor Koch, Roy Cohn, Donald's father, Andrew Stein, Abraham Beame—everybody, in short, who valued his or her association with the Prince of New York City, the Man Of The Hour, Donald John Trump.

"I really started a renaissance here with the Grand Hyatt," Donald exclaimed. "People weren't working. They all left New York City. Now they're coming back, they're all coming back."

Donald's timing could not have been better. While the Grand Hyatt was opening for business, three other major hotels were also nearing completion: Harry Helmsley's Palace over the old Random House site; the Parker Meridien, also in midtown; and the Vista International in the World Trade Center. Following years of decline, New York's hotels were once again prospering as they had not in decades. Prices of hotel rooms were soaring. The occupancy rate was expected to move above 85 percent for 1980, an astounding figure when one considers that 75 percent is robust and anything above is a hotelier's grounds for euphoria. Conventioneers were flooding into the city in record numbers, accounting for 20 percent of hotel income. Business travelers represented another 50 percent. Rooms that had been going for an average of $31 a night as recently as 1978 more than doubled to an average $68 two years later. The lowest-priced single rooms in the Grand Hyatt started at $75 per night at the time of its opening, while larger singles and doubles were $180.

Whether or not one liked the look of Donald Trump's first major building in Manhattan depended, of course, on one's personal sense of style and taste. Some architectural critics thought the gray mirror-glass exterior that projected over 42nd Street was out of place in New York, would be more at home in Houston or Dallas. Others proclaimed it to be sleek and stylish, even if just a bit glitzy. Der Scutt summed up his achievement by saying, "We wanted to create a spellbinding image and have a monumental spirit in terms of architectural scale. No expense was spared in the lobby. The fountain is almost the size of the one in front of the Plaza."

To be sure, the lobby contained enough visual stimulation to keep even a casual gawker entranced for hours. From the pink marble steps and floors, the four-tiered cascading waterfall (that did not burble, thanks to Ivana's supervision), the gold railings, heavy bronze pillars, golden-brown carpeting and sofas, and a suspended brasswork arrangement by Peter Lobello, the lobby was impressive if not exactly a place to relax in. Rather it was an event, a visual happening that made one forget for a moment that the real world was only a few yards away outside the revolving doors.

Best of all, as far as Donald was concerned, it worked. The place was virtually filled from opening day. Out-of-towners especially seemed to love it, to be mesmerized by the sparkle and glitter, and paid premium prices to drink at the bar overlooking 42nd Street and sleep in the oversized beds upstairs. The city fathers loved it as well since they were due for a cut of the revenues. But they did not love it to such an extent that they were willing to forgive Donald's oversight in not yielding space for a passageway between the hotel and the adjacent subway line, as they said he had said he would. Donald claimed that it was only a verbal agreement, not legally binding, and his position was later vindicated by a state court judge. Still, to keep peace with the city, he agreed to a cash settlement.

The only thing that was missing from the hotel was Donald's name blinking in lights above the entrance. He would, one suspects, have liked to have named the establishment after himself, but was not able to because of his arrangement with Hyatt. He did, however, treat himself to a consolation prize. The new Grand Hyatt contains several restaurants. One of them he called Trumpet's and displayed the name with prominence in the lobby.

Even a little Trump went a long way.

37

Politically Donald Trump veered in a different direction in 1980. All his life he had supported Democratic candidates for office, both in New York State and nationally. Now for the first time he decided to back a Republican, Ronald Reagan, for president of the United States. Ivana's political inclinations were more ideological than her husband's. Having come from a Communist country, she was inspired by Reagan's rhetoric and gravitated toward the Republicans. After Reagan's election in November the Trumps were periodic guests at White House dinners and social affairs. Governor Thomas Kean of New Jersey was another Republican who enjoyed Donald Trump's support.

With the Grand Hyatt now opened for business, Ivana directed her energies to the construction site on Fifth Avenue. Donald had said repeatedly that Trump Tower would have "the finest apartments in the top building in the best location in the world," and Ivana intended to see that his intentions were carried out. She presided over the selection of wallpaper, curtains, and other appointments for each apartment and traveled again to Italy to select personally the *breccia pernice* marble for the lobby that was an even more vivid pink than the Paradiso marble in the Grand Hyatt. When some people suggested that the color was a bit outré for a Fifth Avenue showplace, Ivana did not take kindly to the critique:

"What do they prefer," she said to William Geist of *The New York Times*, "the cheap white Travertine that is used in banks? It is too cold, too common. Donald and I are more daring than that."

Nothing less than perfection could satisfy either Ivana or her husband, regardless of the expense. During one visit Ivana detected a narrow gap between the trim and the wall of an elevator. Rather than have it repaired she ordered the entire car removed and replaced with another. Donald was equally obsessed with every little detail. On one of his inspection tours he noticed a hairline crack in the marble in an apartment bathroom. He refused to leave the premises until a work crew removed the offending slab and put in a new one.

The landscaping in the atrium of Trump Tower was of particular concern. He checked it every day to make sure everything was just so. A single flower arrangement out of place was enough to evoke a dressing down. He spent $75,000 trucking a small forest of forty-foot-high trees from Florida to New York. A special tunnel was dug beneath the building to keep the trees from being damaged by frost. When they were finally installed on the lower garden level he decided that they were too overpowering for the lobby and had them cut down with a chainsaw after workers complained about the effort of removing them intact. The sweeping waterfall, a miniature Niagara illuminated by amber-colored lights, was also a sticking point with Donald. By the time he pronounced the effect to be as he wanted, he had spent over a million dollars on it. Later he could state truthfully that he had built one of the most expensive manmade waterfalls in existence.

The hanging ivy that descended on the far wall from the upper reaches of the atrium was another of his obsessions. He observed it intently every day to make certain it was properly trimmed back and not developing a ragged look. In exasperation he turned to Helen Murphy, the owner of Elan, a flower shop in the lobby: "Elan is the name of your business," Helen Murphy told the author he said to her, "and it's also what I'm all about."

He hired Helen Murphy to complete the landscaping for the atrium after deciding that he liked her work best of all. "Donald is as smart as a whip," she said reflectively. "He talks a mile a minute and thinks even faster. He said he wanted the whole lobby to be on the same par as the inside of my store, and that's exactly what I tried to achieve."

With his floral concerns now in Helen Murphy's capable hands, Donald turned his attention back to the sort of activity he loved best after building: seeking out attractive new deals. While Trump Tower was flying up at a steady pace and worries about demolished sculptures were fading, Donald learned that the Barbizon Plaza Hotel on Central Park South and an adjoining apartment building on the corner of Sixth Avenue were up for sale. Once again, he quickened to the aroma of a main chance. Moving rapidly, before too many others found out about the available property, he met with the owners and sensed that they were desperate to unload the buildings. The rent-controlled apartment building was costing them a fortune, and the old Barbizon Plaza Hotel was badly in need of expensive repair work.

Donald walked away from the negotiating table with a signed agreement to buy both structures for $13 million. To put this price tag in proper perspective, it needs only to be said that in less than two months he was able to obtain a $65 million mortgage on the properties, and by 1984 their estimated value was about $125 million. Harry Helmsley, another developer who had his eye on the buildings himself, and saw them sold out from under him before he was able to bid, shook his head in wonderment: "Trump can sense when people might want to get out of a deal," he said, "and he moves in very quickly so others will not get into the bidding and drive the price up. He trusts his instincts and has the guts to act on them."

The clever deal took a different turn later on, however, when Donald got involved in a long-running dispute with the tenants in the apartment building. Claiming that "multimillionaires" were living there and paying as little as "$400 a month for large apartments with park views," Donald launched a campaign to evict them. They accused him of using "harassing techniques," like putting tin over the windows of vacant apartments to give the building the look of a rundown tenement. When he failed to shake them loose, Donald moved his campaign onto legal ground, filing a series of lawsuits against various occupants, trying to get a housing court order to remove them. The tenants, in turn, claimed that Donald was "bullying and annoying" them in an attempt to drive them away so that he could tear down the building and put up a new hotel on the site. The housing court, as reported in *The New York Times* of April 8, 1984, said that the lawsuits were brought "in bad faith," and were "a blatant attempt to force the tenants out through spurious and unnecessary litigation."

In frustration Donald, motivated, he said, by his concern over the plight of the legions of homeless vagrants in the city who were sleeping on sidewalks and in the railroad stations with shopping bags filled with their wordly possessions, offered to house them in the vacant rooms and apartments in his building at 100 Central Park South. At the time the 100-unit building contained ten vacant apartments. The tenants, as one might expect, sent up a hue and cry that carried clear across the city to the mayor's residence. The prospect of having their hallways filled with bug-ridden derelicts was nothing less than terrifying, no matter how much they claimed to sympathize with the plight of the homeless. Trump's real intent, according to the tenants, was to clear out the building in order to get it ready for demolition.

Mayor Koch turned down Donald's request. Donald replied that his offer had been made sincerely: "I just felt badly when I walked down to the park and saw people freezing. Then I looked at the building where I have windows overlooking the park and the apartments are 72 degrees inside. It never made sense to me," he said. "So I just made an offer and it was spurned."

The issue refused to go away. Three years later, with his unwanted tenants still occupying the premises and the number of vacant apartments still as low as fourteen out of a hundred, Donald repeated his offer.

"The apartments are there," he said. "They're heated, they've got hot and cold water, they have the most beautiful views. It's a totally serious offer."

Again his offer was turned down by the city, but the episode evolved into something else several weeks afterward when it was learned that Donald had been approached by a Polish organization that was seeking temporary shelter for members of Solidarity, the dissident labor union, who had been forced out of their homeland. Donald turned them down on two separate occasions, and when reporters called his office they were told that he was "out of town" and could not respond to the matter. One of his spokesmen at the Trump organization said:

"That wasn't the intention of our offer. We were talking about homeless Americans, not refugees."

One commentator, Sydney Schanberg, went so far as to say that if Donald were serious about his offer, providing temporary housing for the refugees would have made more sense than sheltering homeless derelicts, since in the latter instance it was not a permanent solution. A bit of stretched logic, even for an anti-Trump critic. In any event, the issue was still at an apparent impasse at the end of 1984, with neither Donald nor the tenants giving in.

Regardless of the merits, it was an unresolved matter, always frustrating to a man of action and resolution like Donald Trump.

38

When Donald first heard the news of his older brother Fred's death it must have come as a jolt even though it was not unexpected. Freddie's drinking had grown worse and his depression more acute during the two years he had been living under his parents' roof. Fred, Sr. brought him out to the Brooklyn office every day, trying to involve him in the family business and make him feel as though he were an important part of it. But Freddie never did have a head for real estate, never did enjoy the look and feel of the construction site when he was a boy, and now he was immersed in it again at this stage of his life only because everything else had apparently failed for him. No amount of playacting could conceal that he was merely going through the motions, that no matter how hard he tried to learn the business and contribute to it he would never really master it or take to it.

As his condition grew worse and the doctors warned the family that it was becoming critical, they all did as much as they could to save him. But reassurance from the other family members failed to exorcise the devils that tormented him. His physical condition worsened to a point where it became irreversible. His heart was enlarged and, according to the doctors I spoke to, damaged beyond repair. Donald was perhaps more upset over this than he had been over anything in his entire life. He tried repeatedly to reach out and touch his older brother but nothing seemed to work. Inexorably, Freddie slipped closer and closer to death.

He was admitted to the Queens Hospital Center on September 26, 1981, and lasted only a few hours before he was pronounced dead that night. When his remains were cremated a few days later he was less than a month shy of his forty-third birthday. Only the immediate family and a few close friends were in attendance at the funeral. Each one present had his and her own theory about why it had to happen, and what more, if anything, might have been done to save him.

Donald had grown up hearing stories about his hard-drinking grandfather, and now he had just lost a brother to alcohol. His own resolve never to touch a drop was stronger than ever.

Life, they say, revives. Especially new life. Ivana became pregnant for the second time.

About this time the Trumps apparently were growing tired of their house in Long Island and wanted a quieter place to retreat to on weekends. Their friend and attorney Roy Cohn rented a home in Greenwich, Connecticut, the posh community just over the border from New York that they visited on occasion. Roy lived in the back country in a house hidden by trees and shrubbery, but Donald and Ivana liked it better along the water's edge. Both enjoyed boating and swimming and they searched for a suitable place overlooking the harbor.

The coastline in lower Connecticut juts out into the Sound irregularly in a series of jagged peninsulas. The largest of these fingers of land at Greenwich Point is a public beach reserved for local residents; the rest are privately owned communities containing impressive mansions looking out on the water. Belle Haven, Mead Point, and Tod Point are all exclusive enclaves for the super-rich dotted with homes that J. R. Ewing might well be content to call his own. The area that caught Donald's eye was Indian Harbor, snuggled between Belle Haven and Mead Point, and segregated from the rest of the world by a guardpost standing vigil at the entrance. At the tip of Indian Harbor, sitting high up on a hill with a sweeping lawn rolling down to the edge of the Sound, is an immense Georgian manor house made of painted brick. The house was built in 1939 on five acres of some of the choicest real estate on the eastern seaboard. From the water the house looked more like a hotel or an inn than a private residence.

When it was first put on the market the asking price was $5.2 million. Its assessed valuation was fairly low relative to its market value at $858,130, which carried a tax rate of $15,274.71 a year. The house itself was two stories, and it seemed to ramble on forever in a series of sharp angles and abutments. A broad promenade sat directly before the side entrance to the house, which boasted two imposing porticos and a stately clock and tower that soared like a tiara above the slate roof. In the rear was a large enclosed flagstone porch facing the water. To reach the main entranceway of the manor house one needed to climb a short rise of circular stone stairs and pass between two heavy stone columns along a walk enclosed by immaculately tended bushes and shrubbery. A four-columned portico with a captain's walk overhead closeted the front door. The look of the portico and the curlicued carvings above the main entrance was strikingly similar to that of the house Fred Trump had built in Jamaica Estates. It was as though Donald were returning to his roots, except on a scale grander than his father had achieved.

The inside of the mansion was as splendid as the outside. In addition to an awesome array of bedrooms, dining rooms, family rooms, bathrooms, pantries, and kitchen there were separate apartments for the caretaker and the superintendent, a greenhouse, and a half dozen woodburning fireplaces. Three garages provided more than ample space for seven automobiles, and there was a deepwater dock at the edge of the lawn. The only drawback, so far as Ivana was concerned, was that this house, too, was heated with gas.

All in all it was a tolerable weekend retreat. Donald, the master negotiator, managed to pick up this magnificent spread in 1982 for $3.7 million—$1.5 million below the asking price. Sometime later it was reported that he paid $10 million for the house, but Donald said he never gave such a figure to anyone. "I don't know where it came from," he said.

Along with the new princely retreat from the rush of activity in their Manhattan lives came an even more important event for Ivana and Donald—the birth of the couple's second child. A royal family was coming to pass.

39

Work on Trump Tower was progressing smoothly except for an occasional hurdle that threatened to slow things. One of the more serious occurred in January of 1982 when a spark from a heater used for keeping newly poured concrete from freezing ignited a fire on the 28th floor. The flames spread rapidly through plywood casting forms, sending a shower of fiery debris cascading onto Fifth Avenue. One workman was injured but, miraculously, no pedestrians were hurt. The damage was quickly repaired and work continued as before.

Donald was not one to let the grass grow. While his towering superstructure was being built he once again set out on a flurry of activity that put his name back in the headlines and landed him in the middle of some unwanted controversy as well. In March he made a semiserious attempt to buy the foundering New York *Daily News* that had lost more than $11 million the previous year. It appeared as though he might be the leading bidder for the newspaper but, as always, he wanted to buy it with no cash down. Eventually he lost out to Texas financier Joe Allbritton. Donald's real interest in the *Daily News* centered on the new building it was putting up on 42nd Street and Second Avenue. In effect he viewed it as another real estate transaction, but his customary financing methods were not accepted in this instance. Ordinarily he would find someone to put up the money in return for a partnership with him, but it just did not work out this time around.

He seemed more serious about participating in the gambling action in Atlantic City, which is where the controversy came in. When the voters of New Jersey legalized gambling at the polls, the value of real estate along the boardwalk skyrocketed fivefold within a year. By the time the first casinos went up a couple of years later property in that rundown, crime-infested city was worth twenty to thirty times its value of five years before. On March 15, 1982, the Casino Control Commission in New Jersey approved a gambling license for the Trump organization in the record time of two hours. Both Donald and his brother Robert, now an executive-vice president in the company, were cleared individually as principals at the same hearing. To put this in perspective, it had taken Playboy Enterprises some two months to achieve the same results.

There was further controversy when Donald announced that he was leasing land from approximately thirty separate property owners to build a 39-story hotel-casino. One of the property owners was a man named Daniel J. Sullivan, reportedly a former associate of the late James Hoffa, the former president of the International Brotherhood of Teamsters. When the Casino Control Commission hesitated about approving a license for Sullivan (all the landowners involved had to be licensed before the casino could open for business), Donald testified that he would not break ground until the landlord issue was resolved.

Questioned later about his sudden involvement in the gambling business, Donald said that he had had the foresight to anticipate the legalization of gambling in the state before the referendum was passed. According to his own account, he sent something like fourteen different agents to Atlantic City to buy fifteen parcels of land on various occasions; the land acquisitions were made quietly so as not to call attention to his interest in the area and thus drive up prices.

"Everyone said stay away from Atlantic City," said Donald, "everybody but about four guys. I was one of the four. I felt that if the referendum passed it was going to be a tremendous situation."

Donald, of course, had a reputation for being prescient about real estate deals, for anticipating economic conditions ahead of almost everyone else. In his testimony before the gambling commission in March 1982, he stated openly that he was leasing the land for the casino. According to a spokesman for the New Jersey Division of Gaming Enforcement, Donald did not show any interest in Atlantic City property until after the referendum was passed. He then began negotiating for long-term leases on the land in question starting in July 1980.

One of the landlords he was obliged to deal with was SSG Enterprises, a principal owner of which was Daniel Sullivan, whose name surfaced at the Casino Control Commission hearing in March 1982. Another was Kenneth Shapiro, a developer charged by the federal government, according to a *Barron's* report of August 6, 1984, with diverting $65,000 from a Philadelphia crime family to Michael Matthews, Atlantic City's mayor at the time. Shapiro was granted immunity and testified before the grand jury. SSG Enterprises secured a $2.8 million mortgage on the land directly beneath the anticipated casino just one week prior to signing a 99-year lease with the Trump organization. Donald later utilized Sullivan's services to negotiate peace with the labor unions after the Grand Hyatt opened. Donald also referred Sullivan to his personal banker at Chase Manhattan. Chase then offered Sullivan a $3.5 million loan if Donald guaranteed it, but he declined to do so.

While the Casino Control Commission was mulling over Messrs. Sullivan's and Shapiro's qualifications for a gambling license, Donald proceeded with his plans for the casino. In July he announced that he had a partner on the deal. Holiday Inns, the parent company of Harrah's, paid the Trump organization $50 million in cash ($20 million of which went as a fee to Donald), plus a guarantee of $170 million for construction costs in return for a 50 percent partnership in the venture. In addition, Holiday Inns agreed to indemnify the Trump organization against any operating losses for the first five years. The new hotel-casino, Atlantic City's largest to that date, would be named Harrah's at Trump Plaza. It was a classic Trump arrangement: no money out-of-pocket for Donald, and a monied partner to cover the downside. No one did it better than he.

Still, the SSG affair refused to go away. No amount of persuasion on Donald's part could mollify the gaming commission. Prudence dictated that compromise was perhaps the better part of bravado, particularly since he had worked out such a favorable financial package with Holiday Inns. Donald and his partner agreed to buy out SSG for $8 million, with each of them putting up half the money. It was a cheap enough price to pay to put an end to all the negative publicity and snide innuendo.

"I didn't want to be in a position where we put up a $200 million structure and some of the landlords owning a small piece of land underneath the building for whatever reason were not able to get a license," Donald explained.

As if the construction of Trump Tower in New York and the ground-breaking ceremonies for his casino in New Jersey were not enough to keep him busy, Donald began yet another major project at this time. He had assembled a 29,000-square-foot parcel on the west side of Third Avenue between 61st and 62nd streets, and he planned to erect a 37-story apartment building on the site containing 190 cooperative apartments and a glass-sheathed retail concourse on ground level. The entire avenue had become a center of construction activity, but Donald planned to have the grandest, the most unique construction there of them all.

This project, too, would carry his name. His intention was to call it Trump Plaza.

40

With work on Trump Plaza underway by the end of 1982, Donald found himself in the enviable position of having three major projects going up simultaneously: Trump Tower, scheduled for completion within months; Harrah's at Trump Plaza in Atlantic City, with an anticipated opening in the spring of 1984; and Trump Plaza on Third Avenue, which he hoped to have ready by the end of 1983 or early 1984.

The architects for Trump Plaza were Philip Birnbaum & Associates, who designed a Y-shaped building with Y-shaped balconies jutting out over Third Avenue. It was to contain 340,000 square feet of space, 12,000 of which would be set aside for the ground-level retail concourse. A parklike plaza would occupy the grounds directly in front of the main entrance on East 61st Street. There were to be five apartments on each level: two 1,200-square-foot one-bedroom apartments priced between $285,000 and $500,000, depending on the floor; two

1,500-square-foot two-bedroom apartments ranging from $400,000 to $700,000; and one 1,900-square-foot three-bedroom spread at $515,000 to $1 million. Unlike Trump Tower, whose apartments were all condominiums, the flats at Trump Plaza would be incorporated as cooperatives.

In a way, the design for Trump Plaza was a more luxurious version of the kinds of structures Fred Trump had built decades before. The swirl of balconies on the east side of the building would overlook the bustling thoroughfare below instead of the surf at Brighton Beach, Sheepshead Bay, or Miami Beach; and the old aquamarine and flecked-tile aurora borealis motif would be upgraded, to be sure, with a more contemporary dash of sparkling chrome and polished marble. To some extent Donald was doing for Third Avenue what his father would have done for the boroughs if his tenants could have afforded marble instead of tile.

But to his consternation, Donald was not alone in his attempt to bring a more contemporary version of the fifties' high-rise to Third Avenue. He had become such a legend in his own time that imitators were following him all over the city trying to duplicate his efforts. A few blocks further north, on Third Avenue and 64th Street, Milrose Associates (a contraction of the partners' names, Paul Milstein and Robert Olnick) were building their own tower containing 504 apartments and two floors of retail space. What may have annoyed Donald was the fact that Milstein and Olnick had applied for a zoning change that would allow them to put up a 51-story skyscraper. Donald had been planning to have the tallest building on the avenue, and now his imitators were trying to go him 14 stories better. So Donald threatened to oppose the zoning change on the grounds that Third Avenue was already highly developed and taller buildings were not in the best interests of the neighborhood. Some said there was perhaps a touch of irony in the notion of Donald Trump trying to block someone else's request for a zoning change.

More serious was the fact that Donald's own architects designed for another developer a building strikingly similar to his own that was to go up diagonally across from Trump Plaza. Donald's imitators were not only following him, they had him surrounded. The new building in question would be called the Savoy, and it was being built by developer Morton Olshan. Adding insult to injury, the Savoy was designed to hold 234 units to Donald's 190. According to the agreement that the Trump organization had with Philip Birnbaum & Associates, the architects were precluded from using the Trump Plaza design and specifications "for any other building," let alone another one on the same street. Once again Donald's lawyers went into action, suing the architects and the developer for $60 million in damages, plus an injunction to halt construction of the look-alike structure. According to architect C. A. Kondylis of Philip Birnbaum & Associates, the issue was resolved when Olshan agreed to alter the exterior of his building from limestone to a dark-gray glass. "The materials and color scheme were changed," he said.

Four blocks to the west of the Trump Plaza site and a few blocks to the south, scores of workmen were hurrying to get Trump Tower ready for an opening in February 1983. Scarcely visible through the haze of marble dust, their voices were lost in the screech of electric saws cutting through heavy slabs of vivid pink marble. A gargantuan heat blower roared in the atrium, warming the ferns, flowers, trees, and ivy to keep them from dying in the winter chill. Already several retail tenants of the planned forty had their doors opened for business. Among them were Asprey & Co., an English outfit that specialized in trinkets such as 18-karat gold beard combs, mother-of-pearl caviar spreaders, handmade leather cases for polo boots, lifesize silver-gilt cheetahs with spun-diamond whiskers selling for $120,000, ladies' lizard-skin writing cases at $2,000, and eight-hundred-pound American eagles made of crystal, silver, and gold at $230,000. The least expensive item in the shop was a leather key case priced at $100.

Ludwig Beck, a Bavarian firm, was also on the premises before the official grand opening. This establishment offered the public a variety of Teutonic bric-a-brac including forest-green leather jackets with horn buttons for $650, dirndls embroidered with floral designs for $725, lederhosen, Westphalian porcelain, and crystal. By the fall, Asprey and Ludwig Beck would be joined by an international who's who of top-drawer retailers: Buccellati, Charles Jourdan, Mondi, Fila, Amazoni, Botticellino, Locine, Cartier, Martha, the new Bonwit Teller, of course, and many more. The 263 condominiums on the upper levels, ranging in price from $800,000 to $10 million, were 85 percent sold to people such as Johnny Carson, David Merrick, Sophia Loren, and Stephen Spielberg shortly after the building opened. These sales brought in some $300 million, enabling Donald and his partner, Equitable, to pay off immediately the construction loans and mortgages. Since the final construction cost was approximately $200 million, the enterprise was already a spectacular success. They owned one of the most controversial structures of modern times free and clear of all debt, and had pocketed a huge profit. Everything else from this point on was gravy.

Donald had been limited to 58 stories by the zoning board, but as far as the public and media were concerned it was 68 stories in height. Credibility was lent to this bit of salesman's fiction through some creative floor-numbering in the elevators. The 20th floor was designated as the 30th floor, and Donald explained that he was justified in doing this because of the stretched-out height of the five stories of retail space in the atrium.

"There's value if you get more floors in the 60s," Donald added, giving the public a bit of insight into his trade. Some of the condominiums, he said, were selling for as much as $1,400 a square foot, "the highest prices ever paid by man."

The overall effect of Trump Tower depended, again, on one's personal sense of style and taste. If anything, it was even more dazzling than the lobby of the Grand Hyatt. For some, the building was out of place on Fifth Avenue; they were put off by the flashy gold trim around the entrance and the Trump name which was emblazoned in two-foot-high bronze letters on the facade.

"I tried to tell Donald about the value of understatement, like the small lettering on Tiffany's next door, but he wouldn't listen," Der Scutt said good-humoredly. His own reputation was enhanced after Trump Tower opened, and on the strength of this success, Scutt told me, he was able to go off on his own and establish an international reputation.

Others loved the entire look and feel of the building, including and particularly out-of-towners and tourists from other countries. The doormen were dressed in ornamental costumes that made them resemble somewhat South American generals on dress-parade. They wore fiery red coats with enormous epaulets and braiding, dark blue trousers with gold piping down the sides and outsized hats that nearly hid their faces. Ivana had the uniforms made in London and supervised the design herself. She said of them:

"They are fun. Why must everyone be so serious?" She surely had a point, and revealed a most winning side of herself—a sense of humor.

The inside of Trump Tower was another visual extravaganza. The striking pink marble floors and walls immediately caught one's eye. The rest of the atrium was a dazzling display of glass, chrome, cascading waterfall, hanging ivy, and glittering handrails. In the midst of it all sat a pianist in black tie and tails at a grand piano.

"It's become a happening," Donald said excitedly. "It's a great tourist place. People love it. We're 100 percent rented. There are lots of people here, the right kind of people."

That it was a dramatic attraction, there was no doubt in anyone's mind. The atrium was filled with gawkers every day. It was a spellbinding achievement. Donald was right; the public seemed to love it, especially if numbers were any indication. For better or worse Trump

Tower ushered out the age of stolid masonry structures with balconies, columns, and limestone sculptures embellishing the facade. He had brought Miami Beach, Beverly Hills, Las Vegas, and Atlantic City— all rolled into one—to Fifth Avenue. His building might be considered by some to be glitzy and flashy, but it apparently reflects the tastes of his time. Donald's great success is proof of that.

"Trump is mad and wonderful," said Philip Johnson. "I told Donald I hate all that stuff, but people like the show."

"I spend whatever it takes to build the best," said Donald. "Then let people know about it. In New York there is no limit to how much money people will spend for the very best, not second best, the very best." And at another time, on the same subject: "You sell them fantasies." That's how he could get $400 a square foot for retail space.

Quod erat demonstrandum.

41

The actual opening of Trump Tower was not without tragic incident. At two o'clock on the afternoon of May 12, 1983, a six-inch-square shard of glass fell from one of the upper stories of the building, striking a pedestrian on the head. The injured passerby was a sixty-two-year-old man from Pelham, New York named Alvin Gunther. He was taken by ambulance to Bellevue Hospital, where he was treated for a fractured skull. Gunther lingered in critical condition for six weeks, and died on June 27.

A spokesman for the Trump organization maintained that the company fulfilled all requirements of the law when it removed the protective shedlike covering over the sidewalk prior to the accident. The way the law read, the covering was to remain in place until "the masonry is cleaned, and outside handling of materials above the second floor is finished." According to an early police report workers had been seen installing panes of glass on the outside of the structure after the shed was taken down. A Trump spokesman said the glazers had completed their work months earlier. Whether or not this represented a technical violation of the law remained for the courts to decide, but in any case the Trump organization was instructed by the city to extend the protective sidewalk shed. This tragic and deeply regretted occurrence forced Donald to reschedule a second official grand opening for Trump Tower to October.

During this time the ongoing convention center saga resurfaced as a public issue. The project was even more bogged down with cost overruns and other problems than before. Citing his motivation by "pride in the city," Donald offered to step in once more and assume responsibility for the center's construction. He also criticized the architectural firm of I. M. Pei, which had been hired by the city to do the job. "No one has been able to control him as the architect," Donald said to *The New York Times*. "Everything he does is the most expensive."

Donald, it is fair to say, had more than a passing additional interest in seeing the center completed—he had applied for the right to build a twin-tower hotel adjoining the site. But this offer was turned down by both William J. Stern, the head of the Urban Development Corporation, and George Schoeffler, president of the Convention Center Development Corporation, who seemed to feel that Donald's comment about I. M. Pei was an indirect criticism of themselves. Stern claimed that Donald had run into cost overrun problems himself during the construction of the Grand Hyatt, but no one maintained that they were on the same exalted level as those afflicting the convention center.

"If they had let Donald do it, the center would have been built by now," said Der Scutt, who was to have been Donald's architect for the job.

At this writing the convention center was scheduled to be completed without Trump's participation sometime in 1986 at an estimated cost of over $500 million. It will be named after Jacob Javits, the courageous former senator from New York.

Ivana, now an executive vice-president in charge of design with the Trump organization, focused her attentions on the construction of Trump Plaza over on Third Avenue. Pregnant with her third child, she commuted crosstown each day to make sure the construction crew adhered to Donald's tight schedule. The $125 million apartment building was scheduled for its grand opening in February 1984, and she was determined that every last detail be exactly correct, just as Donald would want it. Arriving at the site one morning in the late summer of 1983, Ivana looked up at the balconies protruding over Third Avenue. A flash of incorrect color caught her eye. She dashed into the unfinished lobby and reached for the phone to call Donald.

Pacing in the mud-streaked lobby, Ivana awaited her husband's arrival. Minutes later the long silver limousine with the familiar "DJT" plates pulled up outside. Ivana rushed out to the sidewalk to greet Donald and pointed up to the balconies.

She told Donald that the color of the handrails was all wrong.

Donald darted back to his car and picked up his mobile phone to call Irving Fischer, the chairman of the construction company that was building the structure, and summoned him to the site. When, Fischer told the author, he arrived, out-of-breath and perspiring, Donald confronted him before he got out of his taxi:

"The color! It's yellow, flat yellow, like a . . . like a . . ." Then he spotted it, the color he wanted. "Look," and he pointed. "See that gold Cadillac down the street? That's the color I want those handrails. Gold. Cadillac gold. Not yellow like a daisy."

"We had to go out and buy goddamned Cadillac paint for the railings," Fischer said after the episode was over. "These are things no other developer ever thinks about. They leave it to the architects and decorators. Look, I don't worship at the shrine of Donald Trump, but our company has given up trying to negotiate costs with him. We just say, 'Tell us what you want. You're going to get it anyway.'" He refers to Donald as "the Michael Jackson of real estate. We've been dealing with him since he was sixteen. He was an old trooper at age twenty-five."

With their third child expected early in 1984, Donald and Ivana prepared to change their New York residence, and it seemed only fitting that they move to New York City's "best address," by Donald's assessment: the Tiffany location directly above the real Tiffany's. Donald reserved the premier apartment in Trump Tower, the triplex penthouse with its own whirlpool-equipped marble bathroom for Ivana and his growing family.

"It's a spectacular place," said television newsman Jim Jensen. "You can actually see down into the atrium from the apartment."

Donald Trump had once said that a landlord should not live in a building he owned. "The other tenants find out you're there and they telephone or come to the door at all hours." But he was going to make an exception in this case. America's most powerful and best-known real estate baron required the best address. It was right that he should be able to look out over his empire from the best apartment in the grandest building at the most exclusive address anywhere—even if he owned the place.

42

"I never think of the negative," Donald said, summing up his philosophy of life. "All obstacles can be overcome."

"Donald knows what he wants and he gets it," said one of Donald Trump's competitors. "He has intuition and showmanship. He knows how to get projects off the ground while others are having meetings and doing feasibility studies."

Donald's ambitions at this relatively young stage of his life were beginning to extend beyond the world of real estate. His lifelong love of competitive sports was still as strong as ever. He was a tough competitor on the tennis court, racquetball court, the ski slopes, and the golf course. Baseball had been his major sport at NYMA, so when a rumor began to circulate that he was interested in buying the Cleveland Indians baseball team it seemed perfectly logical. But Donald denied it in the fall of 1983; what he really wanted, as it turned out, was a football team of his own. Football was more than just a sport. It was power and politics as well. It was the action sport of the day, and Donald liked to be where the big league action was.

In September he called a press conference in Trump Tower to announce his plans to buy the New Jersey Generals. The still-struggling United States Football League franchise had lost $3 million the previous season, and there was considerable worry about whether the USFL would be able to survive as an independent league. At the press conference with Donald were J. Walter Duncan, the principal owner of the Generals with a 90 percent interest; Coach Chuck Fairbanks, who owned the remaining 10 percent; and Herschel Walker, who had been enticed out of college onto the team the year before in a much-publicized and controversial transaction. The sale price for the team was reported to be between $8 million and $10 million. Those familiar with the details say that Donald had been able to negotiate a price closer to $1 million. With Fairbanks standing by looking somewhat dejected, a reporter speculated that Donald Trump might replace him as coach the following season. No one denied the rumor.

"I don't know what I might be doing," said the forty-nine-year-old coach. "I'm young and enthusiastic enough to stay in the game."

Herschel Walker said it made no difference to him whom he played for. "I'm a professional athlete. I just go out and do my job whoever the coach is."

Donald then moved the subject into a more sensitive area: "We don't have to stay in New Jersey, but I have every intention of doing so."

Already there was speculation that Donald's chief interest in the Generals was the leverage it would give him in negotiations with the city to bring a football team back to New York. The Giants and the Jets both had abandoned the city for the supposedly greener pastures of New Jersey several years before, and the city fathers, led by Mayor Koch, desperately wanted a team of their own east of the Hudson River. Donald, of course, was aware of this, as was every even casual sports fan in the country. He had just picked up his own team for an apparently bargain basement price and was prepared to spend some money to hire the kind of talent he needed to turn its fortunes around. He was now in a strong position to deal with New York, as well as with New Jersey, when the time was right. He had leverage in both directions.

Less than a week after the press conference Donald denied that he was trying to lure Don Shula, the coach of the Miami Dolphins, to the Generals with an offer of $1 million a year. When Shula declared that the story was true, that Donald Trump had indeed approached him with such an offer, Donald agreed he had but he said he was also considering other coaching prospects in addition to Shula. What followed after this, throughout the entire fall of 1983, was a cat-and-mouse routine that sounded almost as though it might have been written for Abbott and Costello.

Donald approached two other NFL coaches with lucrative offers. When they said no, Donald responded with the statements that he was not serious about them in the first place, that he was just trying to put pressure on Shula, whom he really wanted. And Don Shula now replied that he would give serious consideration to Donald Trump's $1 million a year salary offer but wanted something extra. Donald said yes, it was true, Shula had demanded an "extra sweetener" on top of the salary, but he had no intention of providing it.

What was the sweetener Shula asked for?

According to *The New York Times*, the formidable coach of the Miami Dolphins informed Donald that he would accept his offer to coach the New Jersey Generals if Donald Trump threw in an apartment in Trump Tower, in addition to his salary. If Don Shula was looking to put off Donald Trump, he had pressed the right button. This was the sticking point, the demarcation line beyond which Donald Trump refused to move. He would not bend, much as he wanted the spunky, jut-jawed field marshal of the Dolphins on his team.

"I lost my enthusiasm to continue forward," said Donald, "when *that* was mentioned. That's more than money, more than salary. That's gold."

Donald eventually hired Walt Michaels, the former coach of the New York Jets, as his coach. Michaels, one must assume, had no such grandiose residential aspirations as Shula. And Michaels may not have been the flashiest coach money could buy, but he was a highly competent workman. He could be depended on.

Shortly afterward, when Ivana was asked why Donald, a man who believed in having the best of everything, did not try to buy the Dallas Cowboys instead of the Generals, she said, "Cowboys? We don't want cowboys. Where can we go with cowboys?"

Tom Landry, please copy.

Donald may have suffered a temporary minor setback in the Shula affair, but in true Trump style he rebounded quickly. After losing a round on points, he took a deep breath and came out slugging. Weeks later he very quietly negotiated a deal with Lawrence Taylor, the Giants' all-pro linebacker, to come over to the Generals when his contract with the Giants expired in 1988, and to do promotional work for the Trump organization in the interim.

When the Giants howled up a storm, Donald renegotiated another deal whereby Taylor's own agent had to pay Donald $750,000 cash to dissolve the player's contract with the Generals so that he could re-sign with the Giants. It was a nifty piece of work, one that returned almost all the money Donald had spent to buy the whole team.

"I did this so that Lawrence could benefit fully from his talent," Donald explained. In his opinion, between-seasons was "the time of controversies and raidings."

In this instance, too, Donald Trump was able to come up a winner in the end.

In a further effort to hire top talent to his team, Donald negotiated a five-year seven-million-dollar package with Heisman Trophy winner

Doug Flutie just prior to the start of the 1985 season. In doing so, he turned Flutie overnight into one of the highest-priced athletes in history. Donald was gambling that his investment in the quarterback would return him handsome dividends at the box office. Only time would tell if he would come up a winner here as well.

43

"These units are selling because of the Trump name," said the sales agent at Trump Plaza just before the opening. "When I walk down the street with Donald, people come up and just touch him, hoping that his good fortune will rub off."

As was the case with Trump Tower, Donald's apartments at Trump Plaza on Third Avenue were selling to a roster of international celebrities. Leading business executives, as well as such household names as Martina Navratilova, Dick Clark, Phyllis George, and others, were signing up for apartments. The rate of sale was not as brisk as it had been in Trump Tower, but the magic of Donald's name was helping them sell steadily while units in other luxury buildings along the avenue remained on the market for longer periods. Still, some apartments in Trump Plaza remained unsold two years after the opening, the first sign that New York City's real estate boom of the past several years may have been reaching a peak.

"The Trump name on a building immediately enhances its value by 25 percent," said Donald, and with good reason. He never had had a public relations agent and he did not need one now. He was his own best ongoing commercial.

The Trump empire at the beginning of 1984 encompassed over a billion dollars' worth of property, and this figure would be increased by nearly half as much again when the gambling casino in Atlantic City was completed in the spring. Donald's personal fortune was assessed at about $400 million, while Fred's was estimated at $200 million. By anyone's measure of success, it was a quantum leap forward from the $40 million barony Donald started with sixteen years earlier when he graduated from Wharton.

"Not many sons have been able to escape their fathers," Donald said with some pride. "At thirty-seven no one has done more than I in the last seven years. I have the best diamonds in New York City as far as location."

And nobody was more excited about Donald's accomplishments than was his father. If Fred had to be surpassed by anyone, at least he had the pleasure of knowing it was one of his offspring.

"I don't get involved in his business, " said Fred. "As you know, Donald has a competitive spirit. I don't want to compete with him. He amazes me. He's gone way beyond me, absolutely." At this stage of his life Fred was content to occupy himself primarily with the conversion of the outer-borough apartments to cooperatives.

The Trump organization remained the umbrella for a large number of subsidiary corporations and partnerships, including Trump Enterprises, the Trump Corporation, Trump Management, Trump Development, Wembly Realty, the Park South Company, the Land Corporation of California, Regency-Lexington Partners, Trump-Equitable Fifth Avenue, the Seashore Corporation of Atlantic City, Trump Equities, Trump Construction, and more. Donald even had a branch in Europe to manage the sales and rentals of some ski chalets he had an interest in.

Both Ivana and Robert were executive vice-presidents of the Trump organization, with its headquarters now located on the 26th floor of Trump Tower. Ivana, of course, was in charge of design, while Robert would be taking over the daily management of Harrah's at Trump Plaza in Atlantic City after the grand opening. Robert had grown to the same height as Donald, but he was considerably beefier than his older brother; good-looking but not finely handsome like Donald. He still lived in the Phoenix Building on East 65th Street, Donald's old residence when he first moved to Manhattan. Robert got married in 1984, shortly after the Atlantic City casino first opened for business, then took his wife to Europe for a three-week honeymoon.

Despite the image of a go-for-broke speculator that Donald projected to some, he was by his own evaluation an essentially conservative businessman, and this impression was supported by a banker he dealt with at Manufacturers Hanover:

"Donald Trump appears to be a wild man. He is not. Zeckendorf was spread from coast to coast. Donald stays home. He sticks to what he knows."

Donald gambled on New York City when it was in perhaps the worst shape it had been in since the 1930s Depression. He built his empire because he was in at the bottom and he called the right turns. His timing was just so. He was smart enough to have done it all without putting much, if any, of his own money at risk. He was able to find partners to put up the risk money because they knew he could get things *done*. He had the important political connections in a business where such contacts are a prerequisite to getting anything done at all. He used his leverage well, and was able to manage zoning changes and tax abatements that in the end benefited all his competitors as well as himself. For better or worse, the rules and regulations that govern his industry are different than they were because of him. According to Der Scutt, he was also a master at leveraging a project, a specialty of developers. Buy a property as cheaply as one can, then go out and mortgage it for 110 or 120 percent of the price to transfer the risk should the deal go belly-up. (In the case of the Central Park South buildings he acquired, Donald was able to finance them within months for something like five times the purchase price.) This is standard operating procedure in the real estate business, the key to any successful arrangement. Little or no money up front, then get one's money out, and then some.

Nobody could do it better than Donald Trump.

44

Still, Donald John Trump was not finished yet. With all he had done and all the money he would ever need, he had other projects on the drawing board. Early in 1984 he unveiled a plan, initially proposed to him by the architect Philip Johnson, to build a sixty-story apartment complex on 60th Street and Madison Avenue. The site was owned by Prudential Insurance Company, which would be his partner in the enterprise. When the full details of the proposal were made public, the real estate world was amazed. Just when it seemed as though Donald would never be able to trump himself—not after the controversial structures he had already brought into being—he managed to outdo himself with an even more ambitious design.

This one was truly regal, a pure reflection of the man who was now the recognized king of the real estate world. Donald was proposing to construct in the middle of Manhattan six towering cylinders of varying height, ranging up to sixty stories, complete with turrets, spires, and battlements at the tops. The entire complex was to be surrounded by a moat and access gained over a guarded drawbridge. The name of this latest fantasy community would be Trump Castle, a fitting designation for a utopian fiefdom within the city.

Philip Johnson, the designer of the complex, proclaimed excitedly that it was his "most exciting project ever. Very Trumpish."

Alas, Donald quickly realized that there were limits to the things that even he could achieve. The economics to support such an endeavor simply were not there. The prices he would have to charge to make the project profitable were unsustainable. Within months he and his partner announced that they were scrapping the plan, and instead would sell the land and the existing buildings for which Prudential had paid $90 million in 1981. The asking price was $135 million.

"The question is . . . can you hit two Trump Towers? It was a great promotional idea, but the cost of the site and construction was so much that unless it were a 95 percent home run it wouldn't make any economic sense. I haven't been associated with a loser and I don't intend to be. I don't want my name on something that may not work."

Donald, the old ballplayer, knew that a long out that just misses being a home run is just another out. Part of his success over the years was due to his foresight in walking away from the bad deals before they happened, and Trump Castle was just the latest example. For Prudential, however, it turned out to be a money-losing proposition. The asking price of $135 million proved too high. Within weeks the insurance company put out the word that it might be willing to accept less money, perhaps an offer in the neighborhood of $120 million for the package. Almost immediately it lowered its asking price again to $110 million, and finally sold the land and buildings to a consortium of Japanese investors for $105 million. When one considers the amount of interest that Prudential could have been earning on the $90 million it paid for the site, the sale represented a $15 million opportunity-loss for the company. It was another sobering warning that the Manhattan real estate boom might be starting to mature after nearly eight years of constantly escalating prices. Donald, who brokered the sale for Prudential and earned himself a commission in the process, came away from it whole, as always.

"It sure is easier to get a large commission on a $105 million sale than to put up a castle," said John Baron, Donald's associate, who had ruffled some feathers around town with his evaluation of the Bonwit sculptures three years earlier.

Real estate professionals in New York maintain that property values tend to run in seven-year cycles. Boom and bust, some of them say, have followed each other with almost predictable monotony. This being the case, the city was due for another downtrend sometime in 1985 or 1986.

"I hope I'm wrong, for obvious reasons," said Der Scutt at the end of 1984, "but things could be ready to soften within the next year or two."

"I'm somewhat skittish," Donald agreed. "I see prices that are astronomical. Someday it will all be over in New York. I don't think we're there yet but I don't know. There are other things besides real estate."

America's most powerful superbaron could read the handwriting on the wall more clearly than anyone else.

Donald's dream of a gambling casino of his own in Atlantic City was close to becoming a reality. Ivana, notwithstanding her advanced state of pregnancy, was at the site on the Atlantic City boardwalk almost every day to make sure that the structure was completed on time. She did take time out, though, to give birth to their third child.

Said Tom Pippett, the manager of the construction job, "She delivered the baby on a Friday and returned to work the next Tuesday."

Donald anticipated, wrongly as it turned out, that the return from the Atlantic City casino would be his most lucrative to date. "Take the top ten office buildings built in the last five years, add them up, and they will make considerably less money than my hotel-casino in Atlantic City," Donald estimated. "People don't realize that you need $55 a square foot to break even today."

At the grand opening of Atlantic City's largest casino on May 14, 1984, a surging crowd gathered on the boardwalk and Pacific Avenue for the ribbon-cutting ceremony. New Jersey Governor Thomas Kean was on hand to snip the ribbon at two o'clock in the afternoon.

"During the recession when all of us were worried, Donald Trump decided to break ground and have faith in New Jersey and in Atlantic City and in our future," said the governor. "And I can only say, thank you very much."

There was no way that anyone was ever going to forget Donald's name at a ribbon-cutting ceremony. His thirty-story hotel was built of dark mirror-glass and concrete, and it sparkled like a jewel in the bright May sunshine. It encompassed 60,000 square feet of space containing 614 rooms, restaurants and cocktail lounges, facilities for concerts, boxing matches, conventions, and, of course, a spacious gambling casino that extended throughout the entire second floor of the building. First-day ceremonies were marred when a fire alarm went off accidentally and the premises had to be vacated at 2:40 P.M., but the casino was reopened forty minutes later with a new blast of fanfare. All in all, 9,000 people were shuttled in and out with the utmost efficiency.

The inside of the casino was a pandemonium of hot colors—red, orange, yellow, and purple—brought to incandescent life by a maelstrom of glittering lights and sparkling glass and chrome. In true casino style, it was a far-out stage, a raucous medley of voices intermingled with an endless clamor of slot machines in motion, dice rattling against wood, cards slapping on tables—and roulette wheels whirring on their sprockets. It was a place to lose one's mind voluntarily before returning to the stark sunshine and prosaic reality outside. The most prominent cocktail lounge in the casino, just off the gambling floor, was named Trump's, and the main restaurant in the hotel, which boasted "French Nouvelle Cuisine," was called Ivana's.

It was so many things rolled into one. It was fabulous. It was glitzy. It was glamorous. It was sparkly and showy and fantastic and breathtaking. Some might say it was also tacky, but they would probably not be gamblers. A casino is built for gamblers, after all.

Donald's name sparkled in lights visible from blocks away. It was present in the decals on the revolving doors. It hung from banners inside the hotel, and flapped on flags over the entranceway outside. Harrah's at Trump Plaza might not be the Xanadu that Donald had once said he would build in Las Vegas, but it was a country-fair approximation.

45

Hardly had the doors opened on the new casino in Atlantic City when the first sign of trouble appeared between Donald Trump and Holiday Inns. Donald had been reimbursed $22 million for expenses when he signed his contract with the hotel chain. In addition, to recap, Holiday Inns had paid him $50 million and financed the $220 million construction loan. The company also agreed to manage the hotel-casino free of charge and indemnify the Trump organization against any operating losses for the first five years in return for a 50 percent partnership.

It seemed like an exceptionally good deal for Donald, so it came as a surprise to most observers when it was reported that he was considering a lawsuit against Holiday Inns in the summer of 1984 and perhaps buying the company out and installing his own board of directors. Donald was anticipating record-breaking revenues from the outset, but it turned out to be a disappointing season for all the Atlantic City casinos. Wall Street analysts were lowering their earnings estimates for Resorts International, Playboy, Caesar's World, and other gaming stocks, and Holiday Inns was no exception.

Holiday Inns common stock enjoyed a brisk upward move from the mid-30s to the mid-40s during the summer, then abruptly dropped back again into the 30s during a week of hectic trading. A rumor circulated on Wall Street that Donald Trump had been accumulating the stock—accounting for its big run-up—then changed his mind and unloaded 225,000 shares near its high, triggering a large sell-off. If true, he had apparently decided against following through on any attempt to take over the company. Donald was disappointed in the relatively poor business the casino was doing, and his first reaction was to blame his partner for poor management policies.

Jerry Daly, the public relations officer for Holiday Inns, told the author that Harrah's at Trump Plaza was actually doing better than expected considering the generally poor state of the Atlantic City gaming industry. "It was a bad season for everyone," he said, "but we captured 10 percent of the market share immediately and we were second in revenues only to Resorts International." (Later figures indicated that the casino was seventh in revenues out of ten casinos.) He denied that there was any litigation taking place between his company and the Trump organization. Other factors contributing to the slump in the area were poor transportation to the casinos, with several major highways funneling into one access road, and a maturing economic expansion that was starting to show signs of slowing down.

"When you have two strong partners," said Daly, "these things are bound to happen."

Inevitably, a man as successful and controversial as Donald Trump, particularly one so young and firm in his opinions, was going to have perhaps more than his share of defenders and detractors. Interestingly,

New York City Parks Commissioner Henry J. Stern, the former councilman who had once been one of Donald's toughest critics, was now
one of his staunchest defenders.

"The tax abatement was a good thing," Stern said, reversing his
position of several years earlier. "It made it possible for Donald Trump
to take a risk and build a hotel that started a turnaround of that entire
area."

What about Trump's influence over politicians that enabled him to
secure favors not available to others, Stern was asked.

"It is not a crime to contribute to politicians," said Stern. "For a
New York State real estate developer not to contribute would probably
make him look overtly hostile."

Mayor Edward Koch concurred with Stern's born-again opinion.
Donald Trump succeeded in taking the Commodore and transforming
"a sow's ear into a silk purse. It's important for speculators like him
to succeed so the entire city can benefit."

Others were not so sure. Councilwoman Ruth W. Messinger has
stated that reports that Donald Trump may buy into Lincoln West "scare
me to death. He seems to get his way in this city."

"He's not one of the most enlightened developers," said New York
City's Landmarks Director, Laurie Beckelman, perhaps still fuming
over the Bonwit affair.

To put the matter further into perspective, Trump's and his family's
contributions to politicians have been in character with those of other
builders who must deal with the state and city in developing their
projects; it has never been established, despite grumblings, that any
Trump contributions were illegal or resulted in favoritism.

Nonetheless, Donald Trump was clearly the most controversial real
estate baron of his day by the time he celebrated his thirty-eighth
birthday in August 1984. His major deals had been completed in a
whirlwind of activity compressed into a relatively brief stretch of time.

"I've done it all so fast," Donald said in a reflective moment. "I wonder if I wouldn't have been better off spreading it out over a lifetime. Maybe I'm a bit spoiled. In a way I don't mind sitting back for a while and just seeing what's happening."

For Donald, however, one suspects it had to have happened quickly or not at all. Besides, by striking when he did he was able to take advantage of a depressed economy and participate fully in its upturn. The opportunity would not have existed over a twenty-year period; the numbers would not have been nearly as attractive. Also the political environment might have been less than receptive for him to have accomplished what he wanted to do. It is Donald's nature to do things energetically and quickly. He has a gift for recognizing opportunity before most other people do, and acting immediately. He is not one to sit around contemplating strategy over the long haul—just the opposite, in fact: a man who acts while others are weighing alternatives. It had been a fortunate marriage of personality and opportunity.

Still, with all he had done in so short a period, Donald was a long way from being finished. He might talk about "sitting back for a while and just seeing what's happening," but his mind was already racing ahead to his next project.

46

In a move that captured headlines throughout the country and in much of Europe as well, Donald Trump announced that he intended to erect a 1,940-foot-high, 150-story skyscraper for $1 billion on twenty-six acres of landfill in the East River not too far from the financial district. His tower, said Donald, would reclaim the title of "The World's Tallest Building" from Chicago's 110-story Sears Tower. No sooner had he described his project than an army of critics denounced it as an enormous "house of cards."

"It's a little premature to even talk about it," said Vincent J. Peters, a Manhattan real estate broker. "Anybody who has this kind of dream should go a lot further along first. Otherwise, it's just talk."

Donald described his gargantuan project as a tower filled with offices on the lower levels, a hotel somewhere in the middle, and "superluxury apartments" on the top floors.

In recent history the race to build taller and taller buildings has never failed to set off a flurry of emotional argument and vituperation. From the 60-story Woolworth Building to the 77-story Chrysler Building to the 102-story Empire State Building to the 110-story World Trade Center to the 110-story-plus-tower Sears Tower in Chicago, each attempt to surpass every structure already built has triggered a war among city planners, architects, developers, neighborhood preservation groups, and social scientists.

"If Trump wants to build it," said author Studs Terkel, "let him. We have enough grotesque buildings in Chicago. In architecture, to invert Mies van der Rohe's dictum, more is less."

"The real question that has to be answered is, is there a need for such a building?" said Lynn S. Beedle, the director of the Council on Tall Buildings and Urban Habitat.

"Ego, power, and sensation," were the reasons given by architect Robert W. Jones for the "tallest-building fixation."

There was no question in anyone's mind that the technology already existed to put up such a structure. A symposium of engineers and architects had discussed the feasibility of constructing three 200-story towers in New York, a 210-story building in Chicago, and a 500-story city-within-a-city covering sixteen square blocks in Houston, Texas. If Donald's intention was to inject his own name into the fray, he had succeeded splendidly. It was difficult to imagine what else he could do to surpass himself than to build the tallest building in the world.

"New York deserves the world's tallest skyscraper," said Donald. "I'm only thirty-eight years old. At some point maybe I can build it."

"Going 200 stories or 500 stories high is a marvelous achievement," said Eugene Kohn, another architect. "But I'm not sure what it achieves."

Aside from the aesthetics, the main drawback of such a creation in the minds of many critics was the economic uncertainty. According to some experts, it would cost twice as much and take twice as long to construct a 150-story building than three 50-story structures with the same amount of space. But this has always been true with skyscrapers in the past, and yet they were built for more intangible reasons. Developers have maintained that the prestige of such a building attracts tenants and visitors who would not visit a more ordinary structure.

"I thought I had a site a year or so ago but I couldn't put it together," said Harry Helmsley, who has his own private ambition in this area. "I just keep looking."

Some psychologists, as one might expect, came forward to offer their own rather predictable theories on the subject. Speaking generally about what might fuel the skyscraper race, Dr. Howard J. Kogan declared, "The whole preoccupation with size, the height of a building rather than its rational use, is a suggestion of underlying emotional insecurities. It's similar to a teen-age boy's locker-room comparisons," said Kogan, director of the Training Institute for Mental Health Practitioners, resurrecting the phallic-symbol theory.

Whatever the case, some experts maintained that a tower such as the one proposed by Donald Trump would cost a minimum of $4 billion to build, not the $1 billion he suggested, and perhaps more over an estimated six-year construction period. "To finance it," said Bruce Graham of the architectural firm of Skidmore, Owings & Merrill, "you would have to be the king of Saudi Arabia or some government that didn't worry about interest rates." To many it was inconceivable that there was enough of a market for the proposed 2.5 million square feet of office space and the 1,000 condominiums in the top forty floors to enable the structure ever to make a profit.

"The only thing that makes it perhaps work—and I say perhaps— is the element of uniqueness," Donald has said. "The question is, will somebody pay more for uniqueness?"

While critics bandied about the arguments, pro and con, and city planners discussed such esoteric topics as the "shadow effect" on nearby buildings, "sunshine rights," "wind-shear," the weight of 1,900-foot-high columns of water in the pipes, the "sway factor," air pressure on the eardrums, drafts on the upper floors, overcrowded elevators, and "pedestrian impact" on street-level facilities including subways, sidewalks, and streets, just about everyone agreed that it was only a matter of time before a building taller than the Sears Tower was built. In 1984 twenty-seven of the world's tallest buildings had been put up during the previous four years, and there was no reason to believe that the tallest-building race was about to end. The big questions that remained were, where would the next tallest building be erected, and who would build it? Charles Thornton, a New York engineer, suggested that it would be easier to get such a project off the ground in southeast Asia, possibly either Singapore or Hong Kong.

"In those areas you have the absence of zoning and the economic vitality that leads to such buildings," he said, "along with the presence of big egos."

No one had suggested before that occidental egos had to take a back seat to the oriental, but the basic point was a good one. With American politicians growing more careful about appearance and sensitive to charges that they were beholden to various special-interest groups, it could well have been easier to get a building of this sort built in the perhaps more free-wheeling atmosphere of the Far East.

In the midst of all the discussion the matter suddenly took a litigious turn when Paul Gapp of the *Chicago Tribune*, in an August 12, 1984, article, described Donald's proposed structure as "aesthetically lousy." Of all the words that had been spilled on the subject, this newspaper's were the ones that drew blood.

Donald, via his lawyers, filed a half-billion-dollar lawsuit against the *Tribune*, demanding $250 million in damages and $250 million as a punitive award. "The story subjected me to ridicule, contempt, embarrassment, and financial harm," Donald's suit maintained. It was a "derogatory, derisive, scornful fraud on the public," one that had a "devastating effect on my reputation."

The final chapter on this episode still remains to be written.

47

During all this uproar about the tallest building, Donald did not lose interest in his football team. As mentioned, observers had been speculating that his intent was eventually to move the Generals across the Hudson River to New York City. When he first bought the team he predicted that it was only a matter of time before "the United States Football League enjoyed parity with the NFL." Since the combined losses of the USFL teams amounted to $80 million in the 1984 season, with the Generals accounting for $4 million of that figure, the league was a long way from representing a threat to the financially sound National Football League. Donald had admitted as much himself when he joked, "If God wanted football to be played in the spring, he wouldn't have invented baseball."

There was more at stake than winning or losing games on a football field. An organization called the New York State Sportsplex Corporation was created following the defection of both the Giants and the Jets to New Jersey, and Donald Trump and Yankees' owner George Steinbrenner were members of the board of directors. In 1984 the board voted unanimously to build a new stadium in Flushing Meadows, Queens, right beside Shea Stadium, in order to lure two new teams back to New York. Both Donald Trump and Leon Hess, owner of the Jets, had been approached about the possibility of bringing their teams to the city if a suitable stadium were built.

In the early fall a special state panel recommended to New York Governor Mario Cuomo the construction of a 78,000-seat open-air football stadium on a seventy-acre site alongside Shea Stadium at a cost of $258 million. The panel rejected the concept of a domed stadium, favored by Donald Trump and Leon Hess, on grounds that it would cost $45 million more and would possibly interfere with flight patterns at nearby LaGuardia Airport. According to the approved plan, both the state and the city would issue bonds to cover approximately $112 million of the construction cost, with the balance of the money coming from the sale of box seats, loges, and perhaps a grant from the federal government.

Some critics of the proposal pointed out that the Giants and the Jets had both fled from the relatively new Shea Stadium with its 60,000 seats. Why, then, would anyone be enticed back to a new open-air stadium with only 18,000 more seats located right next to Shea? If more seats were all that were needed, wouldn't it make more sense to spend $25 million to refurbish the old arena instead of building a similar one beside it for ten times the money?

When the issue reached an impasse Donald came forward with a proposal that was at once startling and unique. He offered to build a football stadium himself, without government funding, if the land were made available to him. The stadium would contain 80,000 to 85,000 seats, he said, and it would cost him about $300 million. All the city had to do was supply the land and clear it for construction.

At first Governor Mario Cuomo was receptive to the idea. "If somebody comes who passes a sobriety test and a sanity test and says, 'I will build this stadium at no cost to you,' that could indeed be an offer too good to be refused."

But when details of Donald's proposal were made public, state and city officials were not so sure. Donald's concept called for a "co-op or condominium plan" whereby boxes would be sold for $4,000 or $5,000 a seat to finance the project. Mayor Koch said he would be opposed to any plan that did not set aside seats for the general public.

"It is hardly likely that the Board of Estimate would ever accept a proposal that excludes the general public," said the mayor.

Other analysts found other things wrong with Donald's plan. "Since the seat reverts back to Trump after ten years," said Randy Blaustein, a tax attorney with Siegel, Mendlowitz & Rich, "every year you own it, it loses value. How could you sell it for a profit? It isn't real property, so I don't see any obvious income tax advantages. What happens if someone else sits in your seat and is injured? Do they sue you because you own the seat? Do they sue Mr. Trump, or both?"

Whatever else it was, the plan as proposed was definitely a good one for Donald. The sale of the seats would more than pay for the stadium, the ownership of the seats reverted to him after ten years. There seemed no way he could lose, which was hardly a mark against him. If New York City didn't want it, he said, perhaps he would build a condo baseball stadium in New Jersey, which wanted one badly.

Whatever, one doubts he will forget or give up. Not his style.

48

"We have a speedboat up there, and I like to go out and go a hundred miles an hour in it and come back," said Ivana. "Donald and I are not the type to sit on a yacht all day."

On weekends during the warm months Ivana preferred the quiet of their Greenwich retreat to the bustle of New York City. In her mid-thirties, she had grown a bit weary of racing off to construction sites to supervise her husband's workers. Donald, too, gave some indication that he was getting somewhat bored with all the hustling, all the running back and forth between meetings with his architects and powwows with city planners.

"It's cute," he said. "The football thing is cute and the piano in Trump Tower is cute. But what does it all mean when some wacko can end the world with nuclear weapons?"

Whether this attitude represented a mere hiatus in Donald's life as an empire builder, a winding-down phase after the hectic pace of the past decade, or a genuine change of direction toward new areas of interest, it is too early to say. By the end of 1984 he did start to talk more about pressing social issues such as the arms race, as well as the Trumps' growing involvement in charitable activities. Both he and Ivana devoted more of their time to fund-raising activities: Ivana as co-chairman with Arlene Francis of a Cerebral Palsy Gala; Donald as co-chairman of a Vietnam Veterans Memorial Commission; the two of them together at scores of fund-raising events for photographic exhibits, Great Artists Series, theatrical benefits, and other such affairs.

Their various parties and social evenings brought them into the company of people like Henry Kissinger, Archbishop John O'Connor, Senator Alfonse D'Amato, Gloria Vanderbilt, and Maxim Shostakovich, as well as old standby friends like Roy Cohn and Andrew Stein. They seemed to be everywhere all at once as guests or sponsors of major charitable and social activities in New York and, increasingly, in Washington, D.C.

With it all, however, it is difficult to imagine that Donald Trump could ever walk away from center ring in the real estate world. He might talk about embarking on "substantial non-real-estate deals" such as a television or movie venture, as he does from time to time, and one day he may well branch out beyond real estate and sports into one of these areas. Trammell Crow, the Donald Trump of Texas, is already well along in his own plans for creating a major filmmaking complex in Dallas, and Harry Helmsley has been talking about doing the same in New York for the past couple of years. But whatever else Donald Trump decides to direct his energies to, real estate is what he knows best and it will most likely always be the linchpin of his holdings.

One can picture Donald looking out over the far reaches of his empire from his triplex apartment in Trump Tower, his mind on the myriad possibilities that lie ahead. Wherever the action is, and whatever form it takes, one suspects he will be in the middle of it. He cannot help himself. He has everything, and yet one suspects he is driven to do more. Standing aside and leaving the field to others simply runs counter to his demonstrated nature. His own fundamental philosophy of life is a more revealing insight into the workings of his mind than anything else.

"Man is the most vicious of all animals," he has said. "And life is a series of battles ending in victory or defeat. You just can't let people make a sucker out of you."

Part Five

THE SKY IS THE LIMIT

49

Rumors of marital discord in the Trump household seemed to be greatly exaggerated at the end of 1985, though there was talk of Donald's solo weekends in Atlantic City and Ivana's at their Greenwich estate. In any case, they were still functioning nicely as a team, with Ivana becoming increasingly visible as a spokeswoman for various charities, particularly Cerebral Palsy, and Donald becoming more vocal in behalf of nuclear disarmament.

In the political area, there has been talk that the Republicans want him to run against Mario Cuomo for governor of New York in 1986— an intriguing development, inasmuch as the Trumps have been lifelong Democrats. If Donald does test the political waters soon, it seems likely that nuclear disarmament will be a major campaign theme. In an article in *Manhattan, Inc.* in November 1985, the magazine's contributing editor Ron Rosenbaum declared he was a bit skeptical about

Trump's involvement with this issue when he first heard it, "but," he wrote, "I've come to believe, from listening to him talk about it, that Trump is sincere."

"I have a pilot who works for me who used to be Kaddafi's pilot," Donald told Rosenbaum (a Trump spokesman confirmed to the author the accuracy of this quote). "He's a highly trained American pilot. And I asked him, 'What kind of guy is Kaddafi?' And he told me, 'Mr. Trump, you've never seen a man like this. This man would get onto his plane, and he'd slap his subordinates in the face. A total schizo.'"

Trump went on to discuss his "high-level contacts" in Washington, his growing concern that nuclear technology was becoming too simple and that "a psycho" like Kaddafi might be inclined to "press the button" the next time someone does something he does not like. Whether such talk in interviews is a prelude to a political campaign by candidate Trump some time in the future is hard to say. When the author called his office to inquire about his gubernatorial aspirations, he was told that "Donald hasn't made up his mind one way or the other yet." The indication, though, is that he may be getting somewhat restless with his role as a real estate developer and would like to explore other fields.

On the front of cultural patronage, Trump recently donated the use of his St. Moritz Hotel on Central Park South as the headquarters for the 48th PEN Congress, an international organization for poets and novelists whose American president is Norman Mailer. The value of this contribution was estimated at $160,000.

Ironically, the St. Moritz is not far removed from Trump's building at 100 Central Park South, the locus giving rise to a controversy over possible harassment of tenants, allegedly an effort to displace them so as to erect another hotel. In November, 1985, the tenants at 100 Central Park South asked for a resumption of hearings to resolve their dispute with Donald Trump. The Trump Organization claimed that the State Division of Housing and Community Renewal had already ruled in its favor. Thomas R. Viola, a spokesman for the division, said, "We haven't ruled there is no harassment," according to a November 3, 1985, New York *Times* report. The dispute has grown. John C. Moore III, the head of the 100 Central Park South Tenants Association, has said that Donald is "...a deceitful, vicious liar...an awful man," and Donald has replied that Moore is "...an unsuccessful man who nobody ever heard of except that he's a tenant fighting Donald Trump."

Further on the legal front, matters have not gone especially well for Trump. In September, 1985, a federal judge dismissed the $500 million libel suit that he brought against the Chicago *Tribune* and Paul Gapp, its architectural critic. Judge Edward Weinfeld ruled that Gapp's article was opinion, not fact. "In the realm of architecture, as in all aesthetic matters, what is appealing to one viewer may be appalling to another," the judge said. Some have seen this as a further vindication of the First Amendment of protection of freedom of the press. In fairness, as so often in such cases, truth is mostly in the eye of the beholder—or according to whose ox is being gored. Which, of course, is why we have the protection of a Constitutional test.

Also in the fall of 1985 the United States Supreme Court ruled that New York State's ten percent tax on real estate profits of $1 million or more could remain in effect. The tax had been challenged by Donald Trump and another developer, Richard Pellicane, in a suit against New York State Tax Commissioner Roderick G. W. Chu.

Trump's images—past, present and hoped for future perfect—as in the case of most controversial powerful public figures, are not always at ease with each other.

50

Donald finally did acquire his castle, though not on Madison Avenue as originally planned. Apparently inspired by the return made on his first Atlantic City casino, he purchased another from Hilton Hotels in June, 1985, and christened it Trump's Castle Hotel and Casino.

"I got the castle for my birthday," Donald said when the deal was made.

Getting his castle was not, however, all clear sailing. Harrah's, a unit of Holiday Inns, Donald's partner in the Trump Plaza Casino Hotel, as his first casino was renamed at Donald's request, filed a lawsuit against him, claiming he was reneging on his obligation to build a parking garage at Trump Plaza and objecting to the use of his name at a competing casino. Donald countersued for $110 million in damages, charging Harrah's with mismanagement. Harrah's had projected a cash flow of $48 million in the first year, and brought in only $23 million, Donald said.

"I've given them a Lamborghini and they don't know how to turn on the key," he said.

Harrah's suggested that their ad campaign had turned the name "Trump" into a household word. Donald replied that he deserved credit for making their joint-venture a success, that his previous ventures "... made the name Trump famous and synonymous with me."

Donald's dispute with Harrah's was resolved in his favor in September, 1985. In a sixty-page opinion Federal Judge Stanley S. Brotman denied Harrah's request for an injunction against the use of Donald's name on his new casino. The judge ruled that Harrah's was aware of its partner's penchant for using his name on various projects, and the company was also aware that casino owners can seek licenses for as many as three Atlantic City casinos. Harrah's did not ask for any specific restriction in its 1982 partnership agreement with Trump, and the agreement permitted competition between the partners. Donald welcomed the judge's decision as "... a great victory, a one-thousand percent victory." Harrah's president, Philip G. Satre, said it was a "... first-round victory" for his company since it paved the way for a trial of the suit against Trump. Once again "... in the eye of the beholder..."

(Donald also filed a lawsuit against some non-familial Trumps, Eddie and Julius Trump of the Trump Group, for, in effect, trying to cash in on "my name." Eddie and Julius had been in business for twenty years, using the name they had been born with. Donald was not put off. "I would like them to change their name," he said.)

Elsewhere in New Jersey, to the north of Atlantic City, Donald announced that his football team, the Generals, was merging with the

Houston Gamblers. The new team was to retain the name the Generals and would continue to play at the Meadowlands in East Rutherford, but coach Walt Michaels and his staff would be replaced by Jack Pardee and the Gamblers' staff. The initial plan was for quarterback Jim Kelly of the Gamblers to join Herschel Walker in the backfield, beaching, as it were, Doug Flutie, who ended the 1985 season with an injury. "We'll hold on to Herschel Walker and Kelvin Bryant and some others. We'll have players," Donald said. In September, 1985, there was another report that Donald had been meeting with Pete Rozelle to discuss a merger of the USFL with the NFL; both parties denied there was anything to the report.

If such a merger were to take place, it is entirely possible that the Generals would become the new occupants of a $286 million domed stadium to be built by Donald in Flushing, Queens. It is reasonable to speculate that Donald, who was chosen in December 1985 to develop and run the Flushing Meadow Sportsplex on the condition that he persuade an NFL team to play there, would like to see his real estate and football interests coincide.

Fans of the New York Jets, however, have expressed the hope that team owner Leon Hess, who abandoned Shea in 1983 in favor of Giant Stadium, will buy his way out of a long-term lease there and sign a lease with Trump. Trump seems to discount the possibility: "I would say that the Jets are perhaps not a very likely candidate to leave where they are," Donald said in December 6, 1985 *Newsday* report. "I personally don't put credence in the fact that they may come back. And I say that up front."

Whichever team does finally agree to occupy the Sportsplex—and it remains to be seen whether such a commitment can be obtained soon—the state Urban Development Corporation's selection of Trump as developer of the project represents a conspicuous feather in Donald's cap. The original field of four had been narrowed down to Donald and a development group comprised of Morton L. Olshan, Frederick De

Matteis and Marc S. Ganis, both bids calling for an 82,000 seat, oval-shaped stadium with a structurally supported roof. *Newsday*, in its December 6th piece, reported that two explanations were offered for the choice of Trump. UDC chairman Vincent Tese said it was "on the numbers. It was a better deal for the city and state." Trump's competitor, Marc Ganis, cited Donald's public relations works as the determining factor. "There's a tendency to take what he says as fact," Ganis said. "How he convinced them he could get a third NFL team into the New York market, I wish I could bottle that and sell it."

Donald's public relations apparatus may be severely tested if one hundred small businessmen operating on the stadium site between Roosevelt Avenue, the Van Wyck Expressway, 126th Street, and Northern Boulevard are asked to leave so that the city and state can condemn the land, buy it and clear it for construction. (According to a December 6, 1985 *Daily News* report, Donald has promised to remit fifty percent of the stadium's receipts in the first twenty-five years of its existence, and twenty-five percent thereafter, in return for the city and state's $150 million expenditure.) It is claimed that many workers could be dislocated by the project, including such long time commercial residents as Ben Feinstein, who says his Feinstein Iron Works would be on the fifty yard line of the proposed stadium, according to the *Village Voice*. "My father started this business," Feinstein told the *Voice*'s Pete Hamill. "My son is working in it. And damn it, we want to stay here. But we learned about this in the newspapers."

Donald's proposal to make only half of the Sportsplex's 82,000 seats available to the public has also raised some fuss. According to *Newsday*, his plans call for 221 luxury suites, each containing thirteen seats, to be leased for $60,000 per year; 15,000 seats to be leased for $2,400 per year; and 23,000 seats sold as condominiums for $12,000. In his December 17, 1985 *Village Voice* column Pete Hamill wrote, "Here we are, spending millions on a stadium that's right in the path of airplanes from La Guardia, a stadium that will lead to the dislocation and possible loss of a hundred businesses and several thousand jobs, a stadium that will allow a pack of rich schmucks to get stewed on Sunday afternoon in a safe warm box. If this turns out to be a huge scheme to allow Trump to bring the Generals into the NFL... then everybody should be indicted for malfeasance."

Donald, no stranger to controversy, has, it seems, once again roused some strong passions. Such is ever the price of daring to think and act big.

51

With all his various activities and maneuvering, real estate development remains the field that Donald Trump knows best and that is never far in the background.

When the Lincoln West project turned sour for Francisco Macri, Donald saw an opportunity once again and bought a controlling interest in the parcel for $95 million after the Chase Manhattan Bank started foreclosure proceedings against Macri. In doing so, Donald acquired the largest tract of undeveloped land in Manhattan, the westside spread between 59th and 72nd streets that had once belonged to Penn Central. (Donald said that the property encompassed over a hundred acres; a New York *Times* report placed the figure at seventy-six acres.) Whatever the size, the property became even more significant, being only a few blocks west of Columbus Circle, which was now the hub of some fifteen major developments already in the planning stage.

The plan for the site called for the construction of 4,300 apartments and over a million square feet of office space in as many as twenty separate buildings. There was also an apparent agreement for the developer to make improvements to the nearby subway facilities and a rail freight depot in the Bronx. A dispute arose when some city officials, including City Council President Carol Bellamy, maintained that Donald was obligated to provide the money for the subway renovations; Donald replied that he might come up with the payment at some time in the future if the city agreed to some design changes he wanted to make. Philip Hess, counsel to the City Planning Commission, said the Board of Estimate was inclined to ask Trump for the renovation money before approving any changes. Donald responded:

"If they hold up this project for the purpose of trying to coerce, they would have a major damages problem." He described his new plan for the site as "unbelievable," "spectacular"; "throughout the world they'll be talking about this thing. . . . Because of politics, nothing ever happens in New York," he went on. "This is one of the reasons that New Jersey is doing such an incredible job in its battle against New York. In New Jersey they support economic development; in New York they oppose it."

Donald could afford to sit and wait. On Columbus Circle a few blocks to the east of his seventy-six or one-hundred-acre spread (depending on whose figures you accept), Boston Properties was proceeding with its own plans for a twin-towered complex of offices, a hotel, condominiums and retail stores on the site of the Coliseum. In the surrounding neighborhoods other plans were moving ahead for a multitude of projects—apartment towers, hotels, office space—promoted by other developers, a total of fifteen different projects in all. Donald was in no hurry to complete his own plans. He was sitting on the choicest parcel of undeveloped land. Perhaps he would build something on it one day and perhaps he wouldn't. Perhaps he would make more money by subdividing his property and selling off the parts to other developers. They were bidding up the value of surrounding parcels to stratospheric levels and, not incidently, the value of Donald's land as well.

Then again, maybe he would build the world's tallest building on that parcel of land, something he had once talked about doing on landfill in the East River. During a well-publicized press conference he called on Monday, November 18, 1985, Donald did in fact announce plans to erect a 150-story tower as the centerpiece of a city within a city—a complex of apartment buildings, shopping centers, and television studios that he proposed to call Television City (curiously enough, not Trump City). The mind-boggling development would occupy the entire seventy-six (or one hundred) acres, and contain nearly 8,000 apartments, 1.7 million square feet of retail space, forty acres of parks and open spaces, and more than three million square feet of television studios, offices, and technical areas. NBC had already spoken with Donald about becoming a major participant in the project.

Whether or not this proposal meets with greater success than his earlier one depends on a broad range of political considerations. Donald said that he wanted to break ground by 1987, but the storm of opposition to his plan from local community groups was almost instantaneous. "Since the coalition was opposed to a density of 4,300 apartments, we would certainly continue to oppose a project with a density of 4,300 or greater. I see a veritable walled city," said Patricia Hetkin, executive vice president of the Coalition against Lincoln West. Madeline Polayes, another spokeswoman for the group, was even more blunt. "We will not let you build such big towers," she said. Another critic of the plan, West Sider S. A. Miller, said, "I hope your dream turns into reality."

The main objections to Trump's concept ranged from overcrowding in the area to potential weakening of existing structures because of all the blasting that would be going on to obstruction of some residents' views of the Hudson River. One thing Donald succeeded in doing was capturing headlines all over the world with his controversial press conference. But he confronts a wall of opposition that even he may not be able to surmount before he gets it off the drawing board.

With all this westside activity, Donald had not lost sight of the eastside of Manhattan. In October, 1985, he purchased a ten-story building on Third Avenue and 68th Street from the New York Foundling Hospital. He declined to discuss the price, but other realtors said it was in the $40 million range and that Trump would lease the building back to the hospital until its new home on the Avenue of the Americas was completed. Donald also declined to discuss his plans for the building, but current zoning laws permit the construction of 400,000 square feet of luxury high-rise apartments and street-level retail stores on the site. With New York's real estate market softening somewhat, as many developers feared it would by 1985 or 1986, it is not unreasonable to speculate that he will not be in a hurry to start construction. But one can never tell with Donald. Time and again he has demonstrated an ability to anticipate real estate cycles, to position himself for an upturn or downturn in the market. That he has chosen to go forward at this time with his Television City project may be an indication that the city's boom phase has not entirely abated. Certainly, he has proved the experts wrong before.

While in the midst of preparing for his announcement of the Television City project, Donald had cast his acquiring eye to the south. In October of 1985 he signed a purchase agreement to acquire Mar-A-Lago, the legendary Palm Beach mansion that is something of a mini-empire unto itself, owned by the estate of Marjorie Merriweather Post. The agreed upon price was in the neighborhood of $15 million, and the mansion contains either 118 or 130 rooms ensconced on seventeen or possibly twenty acres, depending on whose figures you believe. Whatever the room count or plot size, nearly everyone agrees that it is one of the most spectacular single-family residences extant. It was built by the Post cereal heiress in 1927, and many of the world's leading dignitaries stayed there as guests until Post's death in 1973.

Donald called it "one of the greatest properties in the United States. ... It is one of the diamonds of real estate. ... It is in a class by itself. To me, Marjorie Merriweather Post is one of the truly fascinating ladies of an era. She had a kind of style that is unique. She was highly intelligent and extremely gracious. I think every bit of that [aura] should be preserved."

Trump's announcement that he intended to preserve the estate intact delighted Palm Beach officials. Previous bidders on the property, ranging from a Houston developer to The Marriott Corporation, wanted to subdivide the land and develop it in different ways. "I want to make sure I don't disturb its special quality," Donald said. "I want to make sure I keep it in a shape we can all be proud of."

Assuming that the deal goes through, one can speculate that the name Mar-A-Lago may be replaced by, say, such as the "Kingdom of Trump."

52

Donald Trump's neighbors in Greenwich, Connecticut, would also have been pleased had he been content to preserve his property—the weekend estate—as he found it. He stirred the natives, however, when in the summer of 1985 he applied to the directors of Indian Harbor Properties for permission to subdivide his land and sell off parts of it as building lots. His application was not approved.

Donald also stirred things up a bit when he approached Joe Keating, the owner of the Showboat Inn just around the peninsula from Donald's retreat, about the possibility of buying Keating's motel and restaurant and redeveloping it. Perhaps the noise from the excursion boats and weekend crowds was disturbing his peace of mind, and if so, the most effective way of disposing of the problem was to buy the place. As of this writing, there is no sale.

Donald was also causing some concern among the locals on the nearby golf courses. One caddy at the Century Club in Purchase, New York, reported that he carried Donald's clubs over eighteen holes as part of a foursome that included ABC sports announcer Keith Jackson. Donald was in a bad mood, according to the caddy, Chris Dehnel, losing four balls. When the outing was over, he went off without leaving a tip. Jackson produced a twenty-dollar bill. If this makes out Donald to be churlish, in mitigation it should be said that millions of fellow link-sufferers can easily identify with Donald's miseries. Golf is a destabilizing "game."

"Donald has a very discerning eye," artist Ann George told the author in November 1985. "When I finished the ceiling mural in their house in Greenwich, he told me he liked it very much but there was one thing he wanted me to change. His eye picked out the one thing in the whole painting that I would have changed myself, but was hoping no one would notice. He zeroed right in on it."

"What was he like to work for?" I asked.

"Let me put it this way. He's very tough, but he knows how to get the best out of people. I can't believe how much I put into that ceiling. I'm amazed when I see what I've done. But that's one of his talents. He gets the best out of you, always pushing you to reach your full potential."

"How about Ivana?"

"She's very warm and down-to-earth, a very good person. She likes having all the money but she's not affectatious about it. She appreciates the art, the paintings, all the fine things the money can bring her. But she's not driven by it."

The author spoke to Ivana in August of 1985. "I would still like to interview both you and your husband for the paperback edition of my book," I said to her over the phone. She was in Greenwich; he was at his castle in Atlantic City.

"I would like to help," she said, "but I have to speak to my husband first. It's hard to convince him if he's already made up his mind he doesn't want to do something. I will talk to him and let you know."

"What does it take to get him to change his mind?"

"Well..."—she hesitated—"I'm afraid he cannot quite forgive you, you know."

"Forgive me for what?"

"For writing his life story first, before he had a chance to write it himself."

53

It's not easy for any celebrity, especially for Donald Trump, to be "scooped" on his own life story. This biography revealed perhaps a bit more about his background than Donald cared to see in print. He prefers to control the kind of publicity and information generated about him. Readers will have a chance to read Trump's own version of his life story with the publication of his autobiography.

Getting his own book out has not deterred him from moving ahead in true Trump fashion on his other interests. Figures released in 1986 revealed that the rents from the commercial and retail space on the bottom third of Trump Tower were generating approximately one million dollars a month, and that he and his partner, the Equitable Life Assurance Society, would realize a final profit of some $87 million when the last of the apartments were sold.

His greatest profits, by his own account, come from his gambling casinos in Atlantic City. In March, 1986 he signed an agreement to buy out Harrah's interest in the Trump Casino and Hotel for $73 million, making him the first full owner of two casinos in New Jersey. Donald apparently considered legalized gambling sufficiently attractive that he made subsequent forays against Bally Manufacturing, the parent organization of Bally's Casino. He bought 2.3 million shares of Bally stock, which he sold back to the company a few weeks later at a profit of an estimated $31.7 million.

Shortly afterward he bought a 73 percent stake in Resorts International for $79 million from the estate of James M. Crosby, the late chairman of the company, and other family members. This controlling interest in the company was protested by competitors who claimed it would give him effective ownership of three casinos and put them at an economic disadvantage. Donald replied with a promise to build low- and moderate-income housing in Atlantic City on land he accumulated if the state gaming commission gave him the go-ahead. Final approval was still pending in the fall of 1987.

Gambling stocks were not the only ones Donald had his sights on during this period. Perhaps inspired by the success of T. Boone Pickens and other Wall Street operators, Donald made substantial investments in the stock of the Holiday Corporation, Allegis, Alexander's, UAL, Pan Am, American Can (now Primerica), and other companies, earning himself major profits in the process. His buying surge brought an article by John Crudele in the New York *Times* speculating on whether Donald Trump was actually interested in acquiring these companies or mostly looking to turn a profit. In his defense, as reported by Crudele in the *Times*, Trump said:

"I've always been a believer in the fact that if a man is capable in terms of a business sense at one business, it's very likely he is going to be capable in another . . . you'll very rarely see somebody who was

252

a failure in one industry who is successful in another."

Wall Street was not universally impressed. One arbitrager, who requested anonymity, summed up his own feelings with the statement: "In real estate he's very successful. On Wall Street he's now considered not a buyer of companies but a guy who's looking to make a buck for himself."

Donald's interest in football was also very much in evidence during the USFL's antitrust suit against the NFL. During the trial Donald told the jury that Pete Rozelle, the NFL commissioner, promised him an NFL expansion team if the USFL would remain a spring league and not compete in the fall season. Pete Rozelle countered to the jury that Donald told him he would build a new stadium in New York if he got his NFL team, and then "would get some stiff" to buy the Generals, according to The New York *Times* of July 18, 1986.

The verdict of the jury was a "moral victory" for the USFL, according to Donald Trump, who not unreasonably tried to put the best light on it, although what followed was the death of the USFL. The jury found the NFL in violation of the antitrust law, but fined it only one dollar in damages; the USFL had been looking for as much as $1.69 billion. The strange verdict gave each side something to crow about, but for all practical purposes it was a defeat for the USFL.

54

Perhaps with an eye on a race for political office later on, or perhaps just revealing the generous side of his own nature, Donald Trump has also managed to build goodwill with a growing percentage of the public during the last couple of years. In the spring of 1986 he offered to take over the construction of the Wollman Memorial Skating Rink in Central Park. The city had embarked on the renovation project in 1980 and was five years behind schedule and more than seven million dollars above the original cost of $4.9 million, and there was *still* no end in sight.

Trump offered to complete the job for $2.5 million (later raised to $2.975 million) by December 15, 1986, at no profit to himself. When the city agreed to his terms he actually managed to finish the job by Thanksgiving, three weeks ahead of schedule. The only hitch—and a slight one—along the way came when Donald erected a sign that read, TRUMP ICE, INC., apparently to remind the public who was doing the job, and the sign was ordered removed from the site. His effort in behalf of the rink earned Trump a glowing editorial in the New York *Times* that called upon the city to search for similar ways of using the private sector to complete projects the city itself could not finish.

Trump also footed the bill for the tickertape parade up Fifth Avenue for Dennis Conner and the crew of the "Stars and Stripes," honoring them for their America's Cup victory in Australia, when Mayor Ed Koch said the city could not afford it. And he came to the rescue of a family in Georgia whose farm was threatened with foreclosure. The owner, Lenard Hill, Third, had committed suicide, and Donald called down to the auction block and pledged a reported $20,000 so that Hill's widow, Annabell, and her family could retain most of their property.

55

Probably the most entertaining chapter in the life of Donald Trump began in the spring of 1987 with a series of events that might well be called "THE DONALD TRUMP-ED KOCH SHOW." It started with a threat by NBC to join other major corporations in their exodus from New York City. Donald offered to sell his $95 million parcel on the west side of Manhattan to New York City for one dollar, with the understanding that he would lease back the property for ninety-nine years, and that his proposed Television City project would be converted to a state-sponsored program not subject to New York City taxes or a zoning review. NBC would become the key tenant on his site at extremely favorable terms with 1.5 million square feet of studio and office space.

The Koch administration's immediate reaction to this proposal was to turn it down. Koch called a news conference to make a two-part counter-offer to keep NBC in the city. NBC would be offered incentives, though less generous than those suggested by Trump, if it renovated its existing headquarters in Rockefeller Center, or moved to any other site in New York, including Trump's. Koch went on to say that Trump was demanding too many concessions from the city.

Trump revised his proposal, offering to give the city twenty-five percent of the profits from the project for forty years in return for a twenty-year tax abatement. Koch responded that it was not the city's business to go into partnership with a developer.

Matters then got really interesting. Trump claimed that Koch's response was "ludicrous and disgraceful." He went on to call the mayor a "moron" and his advisors "jerks." Koch said that Trump needed NBC as a tenant only to attract other quality tenants to his proposed development. When Trump called on the mayor to resign, and said that "the City of New York is suffering, in my opinion, the worst corruption scandals in the history of the city and suffering from totally incompetent management," Koch called Donald Trump "greedy, greedy, greedy," and said: "If Donald Trump is squealing like a stuck pig, I must have done something right."

Was Donald Trump, some speculated, gearing up for a mayoral race himself, or only reacting to Koch's refusal to go along with his proposal? In June, New York State Republican Chairman, Anthony Colavita, said that Trump was at the head of a list of candidates for a "fusion ticket" to defeat Koch in 1989. Trump so far has not acknowledged any political ambitions.

The level of vituperation heated up even more in September, 1987, when the mayor announced that he was going on a peace mission with other dignitaries to Nicaragua. According to the New York *Post* of September 11, 1987 Donald Trump referred to Koch as the "idiot mayor," and also claimed that "Nicaragua may be the only place on earth that's as corrupt as Koch's administration in New York City.

How can our idiot mayor go to Nicaragua when he can't even run New York City properly?" Trump elaborated: "The man is incompetent. After the Nicaraguans see Ed Koch they will lose their respect for Americans, if they had any in the first place."

In rebuttal Koch lowered his voice, saying that the only people interested in Trump's views on foreign policy were "his father, his wife and, I suppose, a few other members of the family."

There was some indication that Donald's attack on Koch might succeed. In September of 1987 sources close to both Trump and NBC announced that NBC was considering buying eight-and-a-half of Trump's ninety-two acres on the west side of Manhattan for about $20 million. At the same time NBC was reportedly pressuring the city to sweeten its tax-incentive package to keep the company in Manhattan. The plan being negotiated seemed designed to save face for both Trump and the mayor since only NBC, not Trump, would benefit from the tax abatement.

"Even though $20 million is not a high price to pay, Trump would accomplish an awful lot from that deal," commented Stephen Siegel, a leading realtor in the New York *Daily News* on September 18, 1987.

The Koch administration was not the only opposition Donald faced in building his proposed Television City project with nearly eight thousand apartments and a wall of seventy-story office towers. Westpride, a neighborhood organization composed of such luminaries as authors E.L. Doctorow, David Halberstam and Isaac Asimov, dancer Gwen Verdon, television personage Bill Moyers, launched a campaign to force Trump to scale down his plans. When Trump was informed of the group's activities he replied: "Everyone's on my side. The public is on my side. The whole city wants it to happen. These are selfish people who live in a beautiful neighborhood and don't want anyone else to experience the good life they lead."

* * *

THE SKY IS THE LIMIT

At about the same time there was some indication that Donald Trump may have his political sights trained on considerably more than the 1989 New York City mayoral campaign. Increasingly he seems to have come to view the whole country, if not the world, as his natural arena. Abe Hirschfeld, a fellow developer and multi-millionaire, announced the creation of a Trump for President movement in the fall of 1987. "We need a proven leader," Hirschfeld said. He claimed that he had already called Donald and asked him if he would object to such a campaign. "I wouldn't stand in your way, is what he told me," said the developer.

Trump for President? Until now he has made and worked his way in virtually every arena he has chosen to compete in. There is no discernible reason for him to limit the scope of his ambitions now. To be sure, the continuing saga of America's masterbuilder promises to heat up in the coming months and year as the various national, statewide, regional and city elections come about. We should learn more about Donald Trump's true political aspirations, or lack of them, in the process.

One thing is certain: Donald Trump's presence and impact on American life will only continue to grow in the years ahead.

__POSTSCRIPT__

The United States today is a country filled with cities that have no history. The newer sunbelt metropolises like Dallas and Houston are shiny ultramodern tributes to man's ingenuity. They are reflections of the high-tech era we live in today, sleek and glittering products of the modern age.

It is in the older cities of the nation—New York, Chicago, Philadelphia, Boston—that the American past has been preserved. Perhaps more than any of the others, New York City was a collection of villages, each a self-contained community in itself. From the Lower Eastside with its concentration of Italians, Jews, and Chinese to the bohemian cafes and galleries of Greenwich Village to the Irish working-class neighborhoods of the East and West 50s to the German stronghold of Yorkville to the broad boulevards of black Harlem, Manhattan Island was always more a collection of ethnic uniqueness than it was a cohesive urban unit. The five boroughs surrounding Manhattan offered more of the same, with each section populated by one or another of the diverse groups that came here from different parts of the globe.

To a large extent this is mostly gone now. Most of midtown Manhattan has been razed and transformed into a homogeneous sprawl of high-rises for upper-middle-class professionals and career-minded singles from all over the country; Yorkville has lost its Teutonic individuality and now looks rather like an upscale version of Times Square; many of the remaining ethnic enclaves are being squeezed into extinction through urban gentrification. Increasingly New York City, as well as the other "museum-cities" of the Northeast, are taking on the aspects of the sleek glass-and-steel metropolises of the American sunbelt.

Whether this is good or bad will be a subject of debate for decades to come. In one camp there are those who believe that a nation that destroys its past will eventually destroy itself. In the other are those who maintain that a nation that clings too desperately to its past and refuses to modernize is encouraging its own decay. The economic conditions that created the immigrant ghettos of the past no longer prevail. People move up, prosper, and move out. Old neighborhoods change or are abandoned, and new ones rise up to take their place. Too often, though, change tends to be forced on people who seem not ready to move. It is not economic reality that brings about this change but the power of city planners and urban developers working together to replace what already exists with the expensive glitter and flash that only the relatively wealthy can afford.

Donald Trump and his fellow developers are at the forefront of the push to change the face of the nation's cities. Among his staunch defenders is George Sternlieb, the director of the Center for Urban Policy Research at Rutgers University. "With manufacturing leaving," he said, "and with federal and state aid diminishing, our cities desperately need the rich. Cities are tending to fall into two categories:

cities of consumption and cities with no economic base. The wheelers and dealers must be successful if New York is to be successful. That doesn't make them lovable."

Bernard Friedan, professor of city planning at the Massachusetts Institute of Technology, views the matter differently. Referring to the development of Manhattan and other cities, he commented, "It is appropriate for residents to ask if developers are being subsidized excessively."

Perhaps the key question is: Is the change that is affecting the cities coming about naturally through economic and social conditions or is it being imposed on the cities through tax abatements and other forms of subsidy? Or, possibly, a combination of both? If it is economic reality that is creating the change, then are economic subsidies necessary to encourage what is already inevitable? Is it appropriate to grant a subsidy to someone who wants to build something if an economic need will eventually bring about the change anyway? Why not let market conditions determine what is or is not needed instead of trying to force or hasten change arbitrarily by subsidizing a privileged few?

The problem is not Donald Trump, or any of his lesser fellow developers. The question certainly is not whether Donald Trump is always likable or not. He is truly a remarkable and gifted individual who would have been successful with or without any help from public officials. Donald claims that it is necessary to move the rules in his favor because of all the planning boards he has to deal with, and all the restrictive building codes and regulations that make it almost impossible to get things approved. There is a great deal of truth in that, but, of course, it is also true that rule changes and special abatements should benefit everyone equally and not at the ultimate expense of others.

Whatever the case, the issue is not likely to be resolved anytime soon. Our cities will endure in one form or another. Donald Trump will endure. And the average citizen will endure too, even if his or her home and neighborhood are altered. We have a history of survival and accommodation in this country, and in moments of crisis and confrontation it is useful to bear this in mind.

INDEX

INDEX

INDEX

Printed in the United States
27920LVS00004B/253

9 781587 982231